About the Author

His Divinity Swami Prakashanand Saraswati (Shree Swamiji) was born in a respectable *brahman* family in 1929 in Ayodhya. He took the order of *sanyas* in 1950. Seeing his renunciation, determination and deep devotional feelings for God, in 1952, he was offered to become the Jagadguru Shankaracharya of Jyotirmath but his heart was drawn towards the love of Radha Krishn so he did not accept the proposal.

Later on he came to Braj and spent almost 20 years in isolated and secluded (*leela*) places of Braj, mostly in Barsana, in loving remembrance of Shree Raseshwari Radha Rani and Krishn. With the will of his supremely Gracious Divine Master, *Bhakti-yog-rasavatar*, Jagadguru Shree Kripaluji Maharaj (Shree Maharajji), he started teaching the path of *raganuga bhakti* (divine-love-consciousness) since 1972.

He is the founder of *Shree Barsana Dham*, USA, *Shree Jagadguru Dham,* Vrindaban, India and *Shree Rangeeli Mahal*, Barsana India.

It was the descension of His loving Master's Grace that only in a year's time *such an extensive Divine work*, "The True History and the Religion of India," was produced by Shree Swamiji which details all the important aspects of Sanatan Dharm (Hinduism) with logical, scriptural, scientific, philosophical and historical evidences.

In fact, it was an imperative need of the present age to have such *a concise encyclopedia of authentic Hinduism* in order to protect and to present the original truth of our Divine scriptures in the world.

Apart from "The True History and the Religion of India" Shree Swamiji has written 9 books revealing the secrets of devotion (*bhakti*) and God realization and describing the detailed philosophy of all the scriptures. He has also written 6 books elucidating and translating the *leela* songs (pastimes and playful acts of Radha, Krishn, *Gopis* and playmates) and the chantings revealed by Shree Maharajji. There are over 300 video speeches of Swamiji on *prasthan trayi* (the Upnishads, Gita, Brahma Sutra) and the Bhagwatam which are shown on cable TV in the USA in several cities. He has thus extensively spread the Divine love message of *Bhakti-yog-rasavatar*, Jagadguru Shree Kripaluji Maharaj in the world.

H.D. Swami Prakashanand Saraswati

Amazing Facts about
Hinduism

Revealed for the first time –
the true history and the Divinity of Hinduism, and
the way it is misrepresented in the world.

Compiled from excerpts taken from
"The True History and the Religion of India"

His Divinity, Dharm Chakrvarti,
Swami Prakashanand Saraswati

Jagadguru Kripalu Parishat, Barsana Dham

Shree Bhakti Dham
Mangarh, Kunda
Dt. Pratapgarh 229417 (UP) India
Ph: (05341) 230442, 230282

Shree Shyama Shyam Dham
158-YA Raman Reti
Vrindaban 281124 (UP) India
Ph: (0565) 2540530

Shree Rangeeli Mahal
Barsana
Dt. Mathura 281405 (UP) India
Ph: (05662) 246235

Shree Jagadguru Dham
Raman Reti Road
Vrindaban 281124 (UP) India
Ph: (0565) 2540057, 2540013

Shree Barsana Dham
400 Barsana Road
Austin, TX 78737 USA
Ph: (512) 288-7180

www.EncyclopediaofAuthenticHinduism.org
www.JagadguruKripaluParishat.org (www.JKP.org)
www.BarsanaDham.org

ISBN 0-967-3823-7-8
Library of Congress Control Number: 2002113952

Published by:
Jagadguru Kripalu Parishat
Shree Barsana Dham, 400 Barsana Road, Austin, Texas 78737
Ph: (512) 288-7180 • Fax: (512) 288-0447

Contents*

Defining Hinduism:

Chapter One: The authentic history of Bharatvarsh since its beginning.

Chapter Two: Hinduism, a Divine manifestation.

Chapter Three: Timeless uniqueness of the Sanskrit language.

---

*For detailed information and authentic evidences related to all the aspects of Hinduism, read "The True History and the Religion of India" which is a *concise encyclopedia of authentic Hinduism.*

Chapter Four: History of the social and cultural developments of the western world.

Chapter Five: Origin and the characteristics of the myths of the world.

Chapter Six: The misrepresentation of Hinduism.

Chapter Seven: The derogatory views of western writers and their adoptation by Hindu scholars.

Chapter Eight: Science of creation of the Upnishads and the Puranas *versus* the modern sciences of the world.

Natnagar Krishn

Introduction

The contents of this book are the excerpts from "The True History and the Religion of India" which is *a concise encyclopedia of authentic Hinduism*. **You should know that the religion of Bharatvarsh (Hinduism) is the direct descension of the Grace of God which is manifested in the form of the Bhartiya (Hindu) scriptures.** Thus, **the history and the religion of Bharatvarsh** are not like the history and the religion of the western world which contains the accounts and the ideologies of the material beings; this is the description of the Divine personalities, Divine acts of the Sages and Saints, Divine descensions, and the knowledge of the Divine approach to God that enables a soul to receive God realization.

Bhartiya scriptures describe:

(a) The omnipresence of all the forms of one single God; His Divine abodes, virtues, absoluteness, Blissfulness and omniscience; and His unlimited Graciousness that reveals His glory, greatness, kindness and Divine love to the souls, making them equally Blissful as Himself.

(b) The origin, evolution and the creation of this universe which is apparently the manifestation of an endless, eternal and lifeless energy called the *maya* that works with the help of God and involves unlimited number of infinitesimal souls which remain under its bondage.

(c) The quality, nature, behavior and the eternal existence of unlimited number of souls along with the cause, nature and the strength of their worldly attachments which keeps them under the bondage of *maya*.

(d) The procedure, practice, drawbacks and the helping factors which are related to the attainment of the Grace of God that reveals His **Divine knowledge, Divine vision and Divine love**, and which makes a *maya*-inflicted soul absolutely Blissful forever;

(e) And reveal the various sciences (Sanskrit grammar and language, cosmology, astrology, sociology, defense and medicine etc.) for the good of the people of the world in general.

It is, thus, very obvious and anyone could understand this fact that the above mentioned knowledges are way beyond the limits of human intelligence; so they must have been produced by God Himself; **and the fact is that they *are* produced by God Himself.**

How Hinduism Has Been Misinterpreted

This is the age of materialism called *kaliyug* that started in 3102 B.C. The effects of *kaliyug* are to despise the Divine truth and to elevate the anti-God elements in the name of God. Its effects were clearly visible since the last 2,500 years when Jagadguru Shankaracharya descended in India. But in the last 200 years such despisations were much greater when the English regime tried to destroy the culture and the religion of India by all means, and, during that time, they deliberately produced such derogatory literatures in huge quantities that confused and misguided the whole world.

Trying to impose the worldliness of their own culture upon the Hindu faith, they introduced such fictitious theories and disparaging dogmas that produced a derogatory and demeaning view of Hinduism. **These publications affected the minds of Hindu writers to such an extent that they also began to think and write on the same lines.** As a result of that, the reputed Indian organizations and world known learned scholars produced such books that were the replicas of the same trend that was promoted by Sir William Jones, the associates of the Asiatic Society of Bengal, Max Müller (who was a highly paid employee of East India Company), and many more.

A Comparative View

Thus, to establish the eternity and the Divineness of Sanskrit language, the scriptures (Vedas, Upnishads and the Puranas etc.), Bhartiya religion, and the Sages and Saints who produced all the scriptures, it is essential to give *a comparative view of the western culture, literature, religion and civilization,* so that the reader could right away understand the whole truth. Accordingly, we have discussed about the origin and the development of the western writing systems, languages and civilizations.

With the development of cosmic sciences and the evolution theories, the intellectuals have begun to think that the creation theory of the Upnishads and the Puranas may be just a casual write up. We should know that our **scriptures are the manifestations of the same Divine power which has created this universe and so they bear the true principles of the creation and the evolution science.** Thus, we delineated the scriptural sciences and explained the initial drawbacks of the modern sciences. **The exact calculation of time since the creation of our *brahmand*** and the authentic chronology with definite evidences from 3228 BC to 1947 AD are also described. In this way this book reveals the authentic form of Hinduism for the good of mankind of the entire world.

May the Grace of my beloved Master
be felt by the whole world,
Swami Prakashanand Saraswati

Holi
March 2003

Defining Hinduism.

Hinduism includes: (1) the true path of God realization, (2) the Divine history and (3) the creation of the universe. Thus, it explains all the aspects of God and His unlimited Graciousness that reveals all the knowledges in the form of Divine scriptures through the eternal Divine personalities (the Rishis). In this way, Hinduism includes all the informations, knowledges and philosophies whatever a soul may need to proceed on the path to God and to experience His absolute Divine love and also to perceive His all-loving and all-beautiful Divine form. *Bhartiya scriptures, like the Vedas, Upnishads, Puranas, Gita and the Bhagwatam etc., are Divine manifestations, so, a Divine personality is needed to reveal their secrets. A worldly mind can never understand their true theme, because, on the basis of his academic learning a person will always use his material reasonings and worldly outlook for the Divine acts* (see p. 61). That's why it is said that (श्रवणं तु गुरोः पूर्वकम्) the theme of the scriptures should be learned from a true Divine personality. Now, we are giving the basics of Hinduism which tells about **God, souls,** *maya*, **Saints (Divine personalities), scriptures, creation, path (to God), descensions and history** etc.

God, *maya* **and souls:** (definition) The **form of God** is **Divine** and **eternal**; He is absolutely **kind, Gracious** and **omniscient**; He is **absolute Love** and **Bliss**; and He is **omnipresent** in this endless creation manifested by Him through His insentient prime cosmic energy, *maya*.

13

Souls are individual entities (unlimited in number) having material body and mind, occupied with the feelings of pleasure and pain and receiving informations in their intellect through perception which is conditioned to the limitations of 'time' and 'space' factors; yet, deep inside they always desire for everlasting love, peace and life.

Saint: (definition) A Divine personality who is always one with God since eternity, or who has realized God in human life with God's Grace by practicing wholehearted selfless *bhakti* as described in the Gita and the Bhagwatam.

Path to God, eternal Saints and the scriptures: (the basic facts)

- God is Divine whereas the mind of a human being is material, having limited capacity and full of material weaknesses.

- **In that case a human being, no matter how much of a genius he is, can never know the path to God on his own.**

- Only God Himself can reveal His knowledge to the souls of this world, and thus -

- To *conceive* **and** *maintain* **and to** *reproduce* **that Divine knowledge of God in this world there must be true Saints (Divine personalities) who could be a link between God and the souls of this world.**

- Furthermore, those Saints have to appear in the world prior to the beginning of the first human civilization to conceive and impart that Divine knowledge to the souls; and because they have to be born Saints so they must have been living somewhere in the Divine abode of God prior to their appearance in the world.

- **It means these Saints have to be eternal Saints, and the fact is, that all these Saints called the Rishis** *are* **eternal Saints.**

⊛ And, because *every aspect of God is Divine and eternal*, the *'knowledge'* conceived and revealed by those Saints (Rishis) in the form of the **Vedas, Upnishads, Puranas, Gita and the Bhagwatam etc., (called the scriptures) is Divine and eternal.** These scriptures describe in extensive detail all the aspects of God, souls, *maya*, creation, and the path of God realization along with the Divine history of Bharatvarsh.

Scriptures: (definition) Bhartiya scriptures are eternal and Divine bodies. They are always in the same form in every age, every *brahmand* and in every creation. (The same Vedas, Upnishads, Puranas, Gita, Ramayan and Bhagwatam etc. are produced every time.) They detail all the forms of God (personal, impersonal, almighty and Divine love) with Their decorations, Their associates and Their abodes (like: Bhagwan Vishnu's Vaikunth, Bhagwan Ram's Saket and Krishn's Golok and Divine Vrindaban). They also detail the class, kind and the nature of unlimited souls; the name and specifications of celestial gods and their abodes; and also the science of creation along with the science of astrology, cosmology and sociology etc. **Their main aim is to teach the path to God for all the souls and reveal His Graciousness.** Thus, to establish the Graciousness of God, to explain the futility of worldly pleasures and to reveal the absoluteness of God's Bliss they relate the detailed Divine history of Sages, Saints and kings and describe the events and the *leelas* of the descensions of God.

Creation: (definition) Creation of the universe is not a coincidental abrupt reaction of some unknown energy as many scientists believe (like the 'big bang' and 'inflation' theories). It is a programmed manifestation of *maya* (the prime cosmic energy) controlled and governed by God. This insentient and mindless energy, *maya*, animated and initiated by God and in coordination with the 'time' energy (called *kal* काल) and the accumulated unlimited *karmas* of the unlimited souls, is manifested in the form of this universe in 12 precise steps (as detailed in the Bhagwatam and explained in codified terms in the Taittariya Up. 2/1). There are two main forms of creation; (a) formation of the first forms of the galaxies, and then (b) creation of the *brahmandas* in it which include the earth planet with the celestial abodes and the abodes of Bhagwan Vishnu and Shiv etc. Celestial gods and goddesses in celestial abodes and uncountable souls on the earth planet are also produced.

Path to God: (definition) It is very obvious to believe that only God can give us the knowledge about His Divine virtues and the path of His attainment; and, out of His Graciousness, He does so by revealing all such knowledges through His eternal Sages (Saints) in the form of the scriptures which relate the path to God in a stepwise procedure for all kinds and classes of souls of this world.

A selfish worldly person has to understand the dire consequences of his bad deeds so he has to become a good and God-fearing person by doing good deeds. A good person has to purify his heart and develop a deep desire to find God.

Selfless good *karmas*; perfecting the knowledge of the futility of worldly pleasures and the absoluteness of the Bliss of God by studying *vedant* (the Upnishads) and deeply contemplating on this knowledge; and practicing the eightfold *yog* according to Patanjali Yog Darshan, are **the paths of heart purification called *karm*, *gyan* and *yog*. They are not the path to God.** A person following any of these paths has to do *bhakti* (selfless devotion and adoration to the personal form of God) to receive the Divine vision and the Divine love of God through His Grace, or one can do *bhakti* from the very beginning to purify his heart and to receive God realization, because ***bhakti** is complete, absolute and the only path that unites a soul to God.**

---

*Detailed explanation of *bhakti* is in "Sanatan Dharm."

You should know that God is one (although He has several self-submissive forms) and the inner desire of each and every person of the world, in spite of their personal, cultural and national differences, is only one in all the situations, and that is *to receive perfect and everlasting love, peace and happiness.* **So, the desire of all the souls is one, God is one, thus the path is only one which is selfless *bhakti* as described in the Gita and the Bhagwatam.**

Descensions of God: (definition) Our scriptures and the descended Divine personalities describe a lot about the unsurpassing Divine beauty, virtues, Graciousness and the Divine abode of God. Out of extreme kindness, He Himself descends on the earth planet to Grace the souls by actually revealing His absolute Beauty, Love and the *leelas* (Divine pastimes, playfulness and the loving acts of Bhagwan Ram and Krishn).

In the Bhagwatam twenty-four descensions of God are described out of which ten are important and out of them only two, **Bhagwan Ram** and **Bhagwan Krishn** (Sita Ram and Radha Krishn), are for intimate devotion that reveals the Divine love of God. Other descensions were only to fulfill a particular purpose. For example: the descensions of the **Divine Turtle** and **Vaman Bhagwan** were to help the celestial gods; Parashuram was to eliminate the cruel and prideful warriors called the *chatrias*; **Gautam Buddh** was to stop the animal cruelty, show the path of compassion and to attain peace (by eliminating worldly desires through non-Godly intellectual meditation); and so on.

Thus, for the loving devotion (*bhakti*) there are only two forms, and, out of the two, the charm of the loving *leelas* of Radha Krishn, called *braj ras*, is supreme, unequalled and all-surpassing. That's why the Devi Bhagwat relates this Divine secret that all other forms of God are established in Krishn and all other forms of Goddess are established in Radha, so Radha and Krishn are the absolute supreme *brahm*, and this truth is further authenticated in the Radhikopnishad and Krishnopanishad.

History of Bharatvarsh: (definition) The history of Bharatvarsh includes the history of this *brahmand* since its origination which is 155,521,971,961,604 years (in 2002). It contains the important events related to the kings and the Sages and Saints along with the descension of God with specific divisions of time called *chaturyugi* (of 4.32 million years), *manvantar* (of 71.43 *chaturyugis*), *kalp* (of 14 *manvantars*) and *parardh* (of 18,000 *kalpas*).

Thus, the history of Bharatvarsh is not the history of triumphs and defeats of ambitious worldly kings as we find in other countries, it is the history of the Divine dignitaries and their affiliated events that form the body of the Puranas which reveal the glory and the kindness of God and show us the path of His attainment through devotion (*bhakti*).

All the scriptures and the Puranas were reproduced about 5,000 years ago by Bhagwan Ved Vyas who foresaw the future rulers of Bharatvarsh (India) so he also described them in the Puranas. Apart from these the rest of **the events of the Puranas are devotionally educational and mostly relate to the Divine personalities and the descensions of God, thus they are all Divine. They describe the entire *brahmand* not only the earth planet, and are related to all the three dimensions (material, celestial, and Divine) and both the spaces (material and celestial).**

This is the reason that a material mind fails to comprehend the Divine greatness of our history because he has only read the history of worldly kings of this earth planet. One has to be open minded to understand the magnificence of Bhartiya history. **Saints' actions are always Divine and Gracious, whatever they are, and a worldly being's actions are governed by his own selfish material** mind which is full of *mayic* defilements. So, an intellectual should never try to draw a comparison between the actions of a worldly person and the similar looking actions of a Saint. (For example: anger of Sage Durvasa was consequently a Divine benevolence, but a material being's anger is full of prejudice and animus.)

Thus, Hinduism is single and prime universal religion for all the souls of the entire world that was produced by the eternal Sages and Saints. Other religions of the world that developed within the last 5,000 years are either the offshoots of Hinduism like some kind of devotion or ritual related to gods and goddesses or some supreme existence or creator of the world; or they are self-created dogmas; or they are based on the local mythologies of that country.

Mythologies and dogmas: *Mythologies are fictions.* They are the imaginations of the early inhabitants of the world when they thought that some supernatural powers were influencing their social living. But, the basis of such imaginations were the stories of the Puranas that travelled in the remote past from mouth to mouth through trade routes to their country. For example: Divine power Sheshnag became the 'world serpent' of the Germanic tribes; Indra (king of gods and god of rain and thunder) and Kamdeo (god of love) became Zeus and Jupiter and Eros and Cupid in Greek and Roman mythologies, and so on. Accordingly they formulated their religious ceremonies.

Pridefulness is a common weakness of human beings. Certain ancient kings declared themselves as 'God' and wanted their subjects to worship them in that way, and certain kings or certain individuals or groups of people created a religious dogma to keep the common people under their domain. Such dogmatic religions or their branches are obviously the products of *maya* where there is no detailed definition or philosophy related to the various aspects of soul, *maya*, God and God realization.

Psychological facts.

Now we are going to tell you such facts which intellectuals always forget. One should know that the receptivity of a human mind differs from person to person. Mind is made of the three *gunas* (qualities) of *maya*: (1) *sattvic* (pious), (2) *rajas* (normally good and bad), and (3) *tamas* (evil) that prevail in every phase and aspect of a person's life. The influence of these *gunas* are of varying degrees on an individual's mind which correspond to the *sanskars* ('conditioned reflex' formed of past actions and thoughts) of his present and past lives.

It is a general psychological rule that each and every thought of a person is imprinted in his subconscious mind as a stable record. They are called *sanskars*. Thoughts can be categorized as: devotional (pure devotion to God called *bhakti*), *sattvic* (all the selfless good deeds, rituals and worship to God with some kind of worldly desire), *rajas* (all the selfish thoughts) and *tamas* (evil thoughts). So, **there are four kinds of *sanskars*,** but for convenience we may say 'good' and 'bad' *sanskars.*

Thus, **the *sanskars* of past lives with the additional *sanskars* of the present life directly influence the existing thought patterns of a person.** So, we see that there are some people who are born good and some people become good during their life. Similarly in the world there are some people who are born atheists and some have become atheists, and thus their mental receptivity to accept God and to accept the Divinity of Hinduism is hampered due to their bad *sanskars. Such people can never accept the Graciousness of God or the Divineness of Bhartiya scriptures. They will only criticize Hinduism, so we have to ignore them.*

It also happens that even if a person, who believes in God and His unlimited Graciousness, if he has read a lot or keeps on reading derogatory (or contradictory) books on Hindu religion, history or scriptures (written by European or Hindu writers or scholars) and has not rejected those views strongly in his mind, his subconscious mind develops that kind of negative *sanskars* (conditioned reflex) and he begins to think (about Hinduism) in the same direction. Then, when he reads or hears about the Divine eternity of Bhartiya scriptures, its Sages and Saints and the path of *bhakti*, his conscious mind resists to fully accept it and gives excuses. This resistance could be from very mild to very strong. *So, to have a fair thinking one should improve the sattvic quality of his mind by positive thinking about God and His Graciousness.*

An open minded scholar must know that truth is truth and human mind has its own inherent limitations and weaknesses; so he must have the courage to accept a logical explanation. There are three kinds of evidences: (1) documentary; (2) inferential; and (3) perceptional or empirical (शब्द, अनुमान, प्रत्यक्ष). In the Divine matters mainly the first two evidences are used. Human mind cannot perceive the Divine matters. In worldly matters although all the three evidences are used but in fact only the first two remain in prominence.

One should know that *lack of physical evidence is not the evidence of nonexistence.* Physical or empirical evidence is weak and is subject to argument. In your daily life if you insist on having empirical evidence for each and everything you come across, you cannot survive even for 24 hours. For example: Do you examine every time that the water you drink and the food you eat is not contaminated? Do you always make sure that your taxi driver would not rob you on the way? Do you insist on seeing the USA first, before buying the air ticket? Do you examine the exact credibility of the doctor who prescribes the medicine for you, or if the medicine itself has pure and non-adulterated contents as it says on the bottle?... No, you don't. In your daily life you live in faith and observe only the 1st and 2nd kind of evidences. *The scientists who spend their whole life in research know that none of the **scientific theories** are absolutely correct; and the **archeological findings** of pots and pans and fossils and skulls etc., could only be the indications of a particular happening at a particular time and place. A generalized theory cannot be derived out of that.*

Whereas, on the other hand, **we have perfect *documentary* (scriptural) and *inferential* evidences and we also have Divine *empirical* evidences of thousands of Divine personalities in our Divine history regarding the Divinity, eternity and authenticity of Bhartiya religion, scriptures and its Sages and Saints which is collectively called Hinduism** (detailed in Chapter One).

Now, what else does one need to know about Hinduism. Even after 56 years of India's Independence (in 2003) why our minds are still so vulnerable that we cannot dare to proclaim the authentic and evidenced greatness of Hinduism, and we are still poisoning the minds of our present generation by teaching them the same derogatory ideologies about Hinduism in schools, colleges and universities? *One should know that Hinduism is not only for the Hindus. It is a universal religion showing the path of God realization for all the souls of the world.*

The Indian government should look into this matter of general public utility and of national importance to protect the ancient heritage which has always been the guiding light for the true aspirants of God's love in the world.

CHAPTER ONE

The authentic history of Bharatvarsh since its beginning.

(1) A glimpse of Bhartiya history* since the birth of Brahma and up to the Mahabharat war.

The authentic documentary evidences revealed by our great Divine personalities (the Sages and Saints) in the form of scriptures like the Upnishads and the Bhagwatam etc. are still available in their original form. They establish this fact that the actual history of Bharatvarsh begins with the creation of this *brahmand* because, in general, the entire earth planet is termed as Bharatvarsh (Bh. 5/20) and, specifically, the land that lies south of the Himalayas is called Aryavart or Bharatvarsh (Manu Smriti 2/21,22) where firstly the Divine personalities appeared and then the first human civilization started.

Bhartiya chronology since 155.52 trillion years.

Brahma. The Bhartiya chronology starts with the birth of Brahma which was 155.52 trillion years ago. The first *kalp* is called the *Brahm kalp.* In the second *kalp* he created the entire *brahmand* with the earth planet. He produced 10 Sages and gave them the

---

*History of Bharatvarsh since 155.52 trillion years and its detailed description are in "The True History and the Religion of India."

Vedic knowledge. Then he produced Swayambhuv Manu and Shatroopa from whom human generation started. In every day (*kalp*) of Brahma's life similar events happen, and every night is the *pralaya* for this world (detail on p. 181).

The existing *kalp*. The existing day of Brahma started 1,972 million years ago; since then and up till today Bhartiya civilization has remained unbroken. Six *manvantars* have elapsed: Swayambhuv (and Shatroopa), Swarochish, Uttam, Tamas, Raivat and Chakchush; the seventh Vaivaswat *manvantar* is running.

Swayambhuv Manu had two sons, Priyavrat and Uttanpad, and three daughters. **Dhruv** was the son of Uttanpad and **Kapil** was the son of his second daughter Deohooti. **Prahlad** was in the family succession of Priyavrat.

The existing *manvantar*, Surya Vansh and Chandra Vansh. Vivaswat Manu had ten sons and one daughter Ela. Surya Vansh started in the family succession of his eldest son **Ikchvaku** whose kingdom was **Kaushal (Ayodhya)**; and Chandra Vansh started from his daughter **Ela** whose son was Pururva. **Parashuram** was born in a distant family succession of Pururva. Mandhata, Harish Chandra, Bhagirath, Dashrath and Bhagwan Ram are the most notable personalities in the Surya Vansh of the **Ikchvaku** family succession that ends with **Sumitra**.

Chandra Vansh. In the family succession of Chandra Vansh, King Dushyant (his wife Shakuntala) and his son Bharat were the important personalities. In a branch of Chandra Vansh there was King Brihadrath who established the kingdom of **Magadh** whose son Jarasandh was killed in the Mahabharat war; and in another branch a glorious king, **Shantanu**, established the kingdom of **Hastinapur** (Delhi). His son was Bhishm and grandsons were Pandu and Dhritrashtra. Pandu had five sons called the Pandavas and Dhritrashtra had one hundred sons called the Kauravas who fought the Mahabharat war in 3139 BC (Bhagwatam, 9th canto).

(2) Beginning of *kaliyug*. (3102 BC)

Kaliyug and **Mahabharat war.** Lord Krishn ascended to His Divine abode at the end of *dwaparyug* and immediately ***kaliyug* started in 3102 BC.** Krishn lived for over 125 years. He descended on the earth planet in **3228 BC.** The Pandavas, after winning the Mahabharat war, ruled for 36 years and 8 months. Accordingly, **the date of Mahabharat war comes to 3139 BC.**

The dynasty of Surya Vansh of Kaushal (Ayodhya) ends with Sumitra (Bhag. 9/12/16); the dynasty of Chandra Vansh of Hastinapur ends with Chemak (Bhag. 9/22/44, 45); and the dynasties of the kingdom of Magadh flourished up to the Gupt dynasty (80's BC).

History of Hastinapur. The kingdom of Hastinapur, after Chemak, was constantly ruled by the people who took over the throne. An ancient book describing the date-wise chronology of all the kings of Hastinapur (Indraprasth or Delhi) from Yudhishthir up to Vikramaditya and was found by the proprietors of the **fortnightly magazine of Nathdwara (Rajasthan) called "Harishchandra Chandrika and Mohan Chandrika" in about 1872 AD.** Luckily this book was saved from going into the hands of the British otherwise it would have been instantly destroyed. The proprietor of the magazine printed the entire description in two of its issues (called *kiran*) 19 and 20 of 1882.

The description is detailed to year-month-days of each and every king who ruled. By adding the total number of years of the four dynasties from Yudhishthir to Vikramaditya, it comes to 3,178 years which is 3141 Kali era or 39 AD, which represents the date when Vikramaditya left this earth planet.

According to the Bhavishya Puran and Rajtarangini, Vikramaditya lived between 102 BC and 15 AD; and according to the above details his period ends by 39 AD. There is only a difference of 24 years in the date-wise record of 70 kings who ruled Hastinapur for 3,085 years. A discrepancy of 24 years in 3,000 years of record could be a copying or printing mistake, and is thus negligible when we are dealing with a longer span of years. *In this way the predicted period of the dynasties of Magadh and the historic records of the dynasties of Hastinapur correspond with each other and justify their correctness, and vice versa.*

The Nathdwara magazine mentioned above gives full date-wise detail of each and every king who ruled Hastinapur from Yudhishthir up to Vikramaditya. **This is one of the rarest records that survived through this magazine.**

❀❀❀

Beginning of *kaliyug,* 3102 BC (evidences).*

We have taken the beginning of *kaliyug* as the fixed point to determine the chronological dates of the events, kings, Divine dignitaries and the important personalities of our history. It is a common understanding that *kaliyug* started about 5,000 years ago (in round figures) and we never had any problems in the past in accepting this fact. But only after the arrival of the English people in India, all sorts of baseless criticisms started regarding our history and religion that were promoted and fostered by them. We had hundreds of such evidences regarding the date of Mahabharat war and the beginning of *kaliyug* in our history books that were destroyed by the British, still we have more than enough material to fully establish this fact.

---

*For detailed physical, geographical, inscriptional and scriptural information about the beginning of *kaliyug*, read "The True History and the Religion of India" which gives 17 positive evidences.

(1) Astrological.

(a) We still follow the ancient astrological tradition. There is a most prestigious, 48 page detailed date-wise journal (*panchang*) with all the astrological facts and figures called **"Vishva Panchangam,"** established in 1925 and published by **Kashi Hindu Vishvavidyalaya** (Benares Hindu University), Varanasi. It gives all the three eras: Kali era, Vikram era and (Shalivahan) Shak era.

It is as thus:

It says that 5,100 years have already elapsed before 2056 Vikram year which is 1999 AD. It means that the existing Kali era is 5101 in 1999 AD, which comes to (5101 - 1999) 3102 BC.

(b) Another *panchang* of India called **"Shree Saraswati Panchangam"** published from Navalgarh, Rajasthan, also gives all the calculations and says that 5,100 years of *kaliyug* had already elapsed before 1999.

श्री विक्रम संवत् २०५६ शक: संवत् १९२१ सन् १९९९-२००० भारतीय गणराज्य संवत् ५०-५१

(c) The **"Vishva Vijay Panchangam"** of Solan, Himachal Pradesh, says,

It means that 5,100 years of *kaliyug* had already elapsed before 1999 and 426,900 years of *kaliyug* are still left. *Kaliyug* is of 432,000 years (so, *kaliyug* started in 3102 BC).

Thus, the best team of the scholars of astrology all over India give the same figures of 3102 BC and publish it in the *panchang* (journal) every year.

These astrological journals are run by a group of the most learned astrologers of India, and thus it is mindlessness if any astrologer or scholar unnecessarily tries to argue about their accuracy.

(2) Others.

(a) **Alberuni.** "Alberuni's India," first Indian print 1964 (S. Chand & Co., New Delhi) Volume I. In the second part of this book on page 4 Alberuni writes, "**...the time which has elapsed since the beginning of kaliyug before our gauge-year, 4132 years,** and between the wars of Bharat and our gauge-year there have elapsed **3479 years**." In the *Annotations* (p. 358) of the same book Alberuni tells about his gauge-year, which is: "**A.D. 1031, 25th February, a Thursday.**"

There is a difference of 968 years between 1031 AD and 1999 AD. Thus, adding 968 years to 4,132 years comes to **5,100 years**, the period that has already elapsed since the beginning of *kaliyug* and up till today (1999), and this is exactly what is mentioned in the astrological journals of India.

Alberuni also mentions about Vikram era (57 BC) and also the Shalivahan Shak era which starts 135 years after the Vikram era.

(b) **Aryabhatt.** The greatest astronomer and mathematician, Aryabhatt, was born in 476 AD. His work in astronomy is an asset to the scholars. He gave an accurate figure for pi (π) as 3.1416. He finished his book "Aryabhattiya" in 499 AD in which he gives the exact year of the beginning of *kaliyug*. He writes,

"When the three *yugas* (*satyug, tretayug* and *dwaparyug*) have elapsed and 60 x 60 (3,600) years of *kaliyug* have already passed, I am now 23 years old." It means that in the 3,601st year of Kali era he was 23 years old. Aryabhatt was born in 476 AD. Thus, the beginning of *kaliyug* comes to 3,601 - (476 + 23) = 3102 BC.

(c) There is also the dynastic chronology of Nepal that goes up to the Mahabharat war.

(d) *Kaliyug* **started in 3102 BC.,** Yudhishthir reigned Hastinapur for 36 years and 8 months, the **Mahabharat war happened in 3139 BC.** When Bhagwan Krishn left the earth planet and ascended to His Divine abode, immediately *kaliyug* started and a catastrophic rain, storm and sea deluge that lasted for seven days, totally drowned and destroyed Dwarika town. *This catastrophe was also recorded in Babylonia's ancient town Ur (which was mythologized in the West as Noah's flood) and the ancient Mayan records. The dates of both are the same.*

(e) **The unbroken chronology of the exact dates of all the Hindu kings of the 4 dynasties that ruled Hastinapur (up to Vikramaditya) since the reign of Yudhishthir is the most potent evidence and it could be easily understood by anyone, wise or dull, so as to believe that Mahabharat war had happened about 5,000 years ago in 3139 BC.**

29

Shankaracharya worshipping his soul beloved Krishn.

''काम्योपासनयार्थयन्त्यनुदिनं किञ्चित्फलं स्वेप्सितं
किञ्चित्स्वर्गमथापवर्गमपरैर्योगादियज्ञादिभिः ।

अस्माकं यदुनन्दनाङ्घ्रियुगलध्यानावधानार्थिनां किं लोकेन दमेन
किं नृपतिना स्वर्गापवर्गैश्च किम् ॥ प्रबोध सूधाकर २५० ॥''

(3) The dynasties of Magadh after the Mahabharat war and the important historical personalities (Gautam Buddh, Chandragupt Maurya, Jagadguru Shankaracharya, and Vikramaditya).

To determine the dates of the dynasties of the kings of Magadh from Brihadrath and up to the Andhra dynasty, we have taken the authority of the Bhagwatam. The currently available Puranas, Vishnu Puran, Vayu Puran, Matsya Puran and Brahmand Puran also give the chronology of the dynasties of Magadh but their descriptions differ to some extent. However, in the first four dynasties the descriptional discrepancy is very nominal and the two important personalities of Bhartiya history, **Buddh** and **Chandragupt Maurya**, happened to be during this period. For Gupt dynasty, which comes after Andhra dynasty, and for the individual reigning periods of certain kings of **Shishunag** and **Maurya dynasty**, we have taken the figures of Kaliyug Rajvrittant of Bhavishya Puran which still survives in Narayana Sastry's works.

The Bhagwatam doesn't give the details of the ninth Gupt dynasty. It only says 'the seven Abhiras' which means the seven kings will be of the subordinate class of people.

We have taken its details from Kaliyug Rajvrittant. There were seven kings in the **Gupt dynasty**: (1) Chandragupt Vijayaditya (ruling period 7 years), (2) Samudragupt Ashokaditya Priyadarshin (51 years), (3) Chandragupt II Vikramaditya (36 years), (4) Kumargupt Mahendraditya (42 years), (5) Skandgupt Parakramaditya (25 years), (6) Nrasinghgupt Baladitya (40 years) and (7) Kumargupt II Vikramaditya (44 years). The total reigning period was 245 years. **Thus, the total number of years of all the nine dynasties of Magadh (from Brihadrath to Andhra and Gupt) is 2,811 + 245 = 3,056 years, which comes to (3139 - 3056) 83 BC (see chart on p. 40).**

❦❦❦

Gautam Buddh (b. 1894 BC - d. 1814 BC).

After his 49 days austerity, Gautam Buddh discovered that 'desires' are the only cause of all the pains so they have to be totally removed to make one happy. He was now thirty-five. He then proceeded to Varanasi and started preaching his religion. In his last days he also visited Vaishali. **He lived for 80 years.**

The Mahabharat war had happened in 3139 BC and, according to the Bhagwatam, after the war Brihadrath dynasty ruled for about 1,000 years. Pradyot dynasty for 138 years, and then it was taken over by Shishunag dynasty. The fifth king of Shishunag dynasty was Bimbsar. **It is a well known historical fact that Gautam Buddh was propagating his religion during the reigning period of King Bimbsar.**

In the Shishunag dynasty (according to Kaliyug Rajvrittant) Shishunag ruled for 40 years, Kakvarn 36, Chem Dharma 26 and Chamoja 40 years, then Bimbsar took over the throne and ruled for 38 years. Thus, deducting [1,000+138+142 (40+36+26+40)] 1,280 years from 3139 comes to 1859 BC. Now adding 35 years of Buddh's existing age of that time to 1859 comes to 1894 BC which is the birth date of Buddh.

Again, *the Buddhist records say that he was already 72 years old at the time of Ajatshatnu's coronation;* it means that he was in his 73rd year at that time. Shishunag dynasty's period is 2001 BC to 1641 BC. The five kings, Shishunag to Bindusar, ruled for (40+36+26+40+38) 180 years. Then Ajatshatnu became the king and ruled for 27 years. Accordingly, 2001 BC (-) 180 = 1821 BC is the coronation year of Ajatshatnu. Adding 73 years (the existing age of Gautam Buddh at that time) to 1821 BC comes to 1894 BC. Thus, according to Buddhist records also, **the date of birth of Gautam Buddh is 1894 BC and his *nirvan* year is (1894-80) 1814 BC.** He was born on Vaishakh full moon day which is March/April.

❀❀❀

Chandragupt Maurya (1541 BC - 1507 BC).

He was the first king of the fourth dynasty of Magadh. His mother's name was Mur, so he was called Maurya in Sanskrit which means the son of Mur, and thus, his dynasty was called Maurya dynasty. A pious, learned and determined *brahman*, Chanakya, also known as Kautilya, who had an intelligent brain, managed to terminate the existing King Mahapadm Nand and his eight sons and made Chandragupt the King of Magadh who was also the legitimate heir of the throne. The total period of the four dynasties including the Nand dynasty after the Mahabharat war is 1,598 years (1,000 + 138 + 360 + 100). **Thus, the coronation date of Chandragupt Maurya comes to 3139 - 1598 = 1541 BC.**

Chandragupt Maurya ruled for 34 years (1541-1507 BC), his son Bindusar ruled 28 years (1507-1479 BC) and his grandson Ashokvardhan ruled for 36 years (1479-1443 BC).

❀❀❀

Jagadguru Shankaracharya (509 - 477 BC).

The most efficient documentary evidence of Shankaracharya's period is the carefully preserved date-wise list of all the succeeding Shankaracharyas who sat on that religious throne which was established by Adi (the original) Shankaracharya thousands of years ago; **and that list goes back up to 477 BC. Adi Shankaracharya lived only 32 years so his birth date is 477 + 32 = 509 BC. He** had established four *maths.* (*Math* is a religious throne, which is used as a center for propagating *dharm,* and whoever sits on that throne, holds the title of Shankaracharya.) In his last days, Adi

Shankaracharya lived in Kanchi Kamkoti so it is also considered as a *math*. **Dwarika Sharda Math and Kanchi Kamkoti Math, both have the complete date-wise record of all the succeeding Shankaracharyas for the last 2,500** years, but the records of Kanchi Math are more detailed.

Shankaracharya established four *peeth* (*math*) and appointed four *sanyasi* disciples at those *peeth* as *acharyas*.

Jyotishpeeth at Badrikashram (also called Jyotirmath)	Totakacharya
Sharda Peeth at Dwarika (also called Dwarika Sharda Math)	Sureshwaracharya
Sringeri Peeth, South India (also called Sringeri Math)	Hastamalakacharya
Govardhan Peeth at Puri (also called Govardhan Math)	Padmpadacharya

Shankaracharya, after establishing the four *maths* and spreading the greatness of Sanatan Dharm, came back to South India and, for the last four to six years of his life, he lived in Kanchi Kamkoti. Thus, Kanchi Kamkoti is called the fifth *math*.

Thus, according to the records of Kanchi Kamkoti Math, Adi Shankaracharya was born on 2593 Kali era and left this earth planet on 2625 Kali era which comes to (3102 - 2593) 509 BC and (3102 - 2625) 477 BC. The same dates are mentioned in the records of Dwarika Sharda Math except that they are written in Yudhishthir era.

Vikramaditya (102 BC - 15 AD)

Bhavishya Puran. Vikram era started in 57 BC by **Vikramaditya the Great** as a commemoration of his victory upon the Shaks. There is plentiful literature on Vikramaditya, and in the

Bhavishya Puran itself there are descriptions of Vikramaditya in more than 40 chapters between Pratisarg Parv I and IV. He was a descended Divine personality. His capital was Ujjain where the famous temple of Mahakaleshwar exists. Pratisarg Parv IV, chapter 1 of Bhavishya Puran says that after the elapse of a full 3,000 years in *kaliyug* (3102 - 3000 = 102 BC), a dynamic Divine personality was born who was named Vikramaditya. He was very intelligent and loving to his parents. When he was only five years old he went into the jungles to worship God. After twelve years, when he came out, God Shiv sent for him a celestial golden throne which was decorated with thirty-two statues. He then came (to Ujjain), adored Mahakaleshwar (God Shiv) and established an elegant shrine.

Bhavishya Puran further says that **the great King Vikramaditya ruled for one hundred years.** Then his son Deobhakt ruled for ten years **and his grandson Shalivahan, who established Shalivahan Shak era (in 78 AD), defeated the Shaks and ruled for sixty years.** Vikramaditya belonged to Pramar dynasty in which there was another very powerful King, Bhojraj, who was eleven generations later than Shalivahan. The Pramar dynasty (which ends with Ganga Singh) is described in the first chapter of Pratisarg Parv IV.

According to the above descriptions Vikramaditya lived for (5 years + 12 years + 100 years) 117 years (102 BC to 15 AD).

Bhagwan Krishn

(4) Summary and the chronological chart since 3228 BC.

To sum up: The dynastic dates of the kings of Hastinapur are the actual historic records, but the dynasties of Magadh given in the Bhagwatam or Bhavishya Puran are the predictions by the descended Divine personality Ved Vyas who reproduced all the Vedas and Puranas before 3102 BC. The dynastic periods of both, Hastinapur and Magadh, (up to Vikramaditya) coincide with only a difference of 24 years in 3,000 years of records which is almost negligible.

It was the greatness of the predictions that all the events of the history happened the same way as predicted. There could be a difference of a few years (but not in hundreds) in the actual dynastic dates of the individual kings and the predicted dates, because the actual historic happening is also affected by the accumulated existing *karmas* and the general quality of the consciousness of the people of the world. So there is a likelihood of some difference, but not a lot.

Total number of years of the first eight dynasties of Magadh is 2,811 years. Adding 245 years of the ninth Gupt dynasty comes to 3,056 years from the Mahabharat war which is (3139 - 3056) 83 BC.

After the downfall of Gupt dynasty the kingship of Magadh ended and it went under the subordination of Vikramaditya of Ujjain (Malva). Although the kings of Gupt family had defeated the Huns several times, the Shaks were still powerful in their attacks. They were finally defeated by Vikramaditya, and thus **the Vikram era was established in 57 BC.** Another powerful king, Shalivahan, again abolished the Shaks from India, and, in this way, the **Shalivahan Shak era started in 78 AD. After that, the regal power of India was divided into several kingships and the Rajpoot kings ruled India for 1,107 years when Mohammad Gori invaded Delhi (Hastinapur) in 1192 AD and became the king.**

That was the period when a number of stories of the bravery and sincerity of the Rajpoots were composed and were enthusiastically sung as folklore in the towns and the villages, and many history books were also written at that time, out of which only a few are available nowadays. The rest of them filled the trash bins of the British rulers of those days.

When Muslims took over Delhi, they started to suppress Hindu religion and faith. They ruled for 565 years when in 1757 Clive's forces crushed and killed the Nawab and in this way the British regime was established in Bengal, the richest province of India.

The British had come to India (Calcutta) as traders (East India Co.) in 1690 and, with their diplomatic skill, they established their regime in 1757, starting from Calcutta (Bengal) and spreading up to Benares, Mysore and Poona. It evoked the patriotism of Indian souls that resulted in the general revolution for independence in 1857. But, because of certain internal reasons, it didn't succeed and it resulted into a full fledged British rule that dignified the Queen with the title of the Empress of India. Then, the English education was preferred which was designed to passively induce their beliefs in our educated community.

In 1918, however, an agreement was drawn to solace the burning hearts of the Indians demanding the independence of India with a promise to start a democratic rule, but it was never properly implemented and the second world war broke out in 1939, shaking the whole world and exhausting the 'friendly nations' (India, England and France) for six years. It resulted in a state of despair for the British to reconstruct the damages of their own country, and thus, they had to leave India after 190 years of their rule by favoring us with the independence which they declared on August 15, 1947. They took some time to finish the paperwork and finally left India on January 26, 1948. Now (in 2002) it is the 55th year of India's independence. Thus, we briefly described the history of India from the Mahabharat war up till today.

The Bhagwatam (*mahatmya,* chapter six) says that after the ascension of Krishn and the elapse of thirty years of *kaliyug,* on the ninth waxing moon day of Bhadrapad (which is September 3072 BC) foremost *gyani* Saint, Shukdeo, from his Divine memory, started explaining the Bhagwatam. After 200 years of the elapse of *kaliyug,* Saint Gokarn again recited and explained the Bhagwatam in the month of Asadh (July); and after 230 years of the elapse of *kaliyug,* Sankadik Paramhans started relating the Bhagwatam on the ninth waxing day of Kartik which is October 2842 BC. This documentary evidence is enough for an open minded scholar to understand that our scriptures are Divine manifestations that were produced for the good of mankind.

Shukdeo Paramhans relating the Bhagwatam to Parikchit
along with the Sages and Saints (3072 BC).

Chronology of the Indian History since 3228 BC

3228	Descension of **Bhagwan Krishn**.*
3139	The Mahabharat war (lasted for 18 days). Beginning of **Brihadrath** dynasty of **Magadh**, and **Yudhishthir** dynasty of **Hastinapur**. (Brihadrath dynasty starts with Marjari so it is also called the dynasty of Marjari family.)
3102	Ascension of Bhagwan Krishn and the beginning of *kaliyug*.**
2139	End of Brihadrath dynasty (21 kings for 1,000 years).
2139-2001	**Pradyot** dynasty (5 kings for 138 years).
2001-1641	**Shishunag** dynasty (10 kings for 360 years).
1894-1814	**Gautam Buddh.**
1641-1541	**Nandas** (Mahapadm Nand and his 8 sons for 100 years).
1541-1241	**Maurya** dynasty (10 kings for about 300 years).
1541-1507	**Chandragupt Maurya** (34 years).
1507-1479	Bindusar (28 years).

---

*In the **Bhagwatam**, Brahma tells in round figures that Krishn remained on this earth planet for 125 years (यदुवंशेऽवतीर्णस्य भवतः पुरुषोत्तम । शरच्छतं व्यतीयाय पञ्चविंशाधिकं प्रभो ॥ ११/६/२५). Accordingly, if you add 125 years to February 3102, if comes to February 3227 BC. But Krishn's descension was in the Rohini *nakchatra* (asterism) of the 8th waning moon midnight of *bhadon* (August) which is about seven months earlier. Thus, His descension date is 3228 BC and He stayed on the earth planet for 125 year and about 7 months.

According to the **"Surya Siddhant" the astrologers have calculated that *kaliyug* started on the afternoon of 17th February, 3102 BC.

1479-1443	**Ashokvardhan** (36 years).
1241-784	**Shung** and **Kanua** dynasty (14 kings for 457 years).
784-328	**Andhra** dynasty (30 kings for 456 years).
509-477	**Jagadguru Shankaracharya.**
328-83	**Gupt** dynasty (7 kings for 245 years).
	(Chandragupt Vijayaditya, 328-321 BC, and Alexander's invasion was 326 BC.)
	(Samudragupt Ashokaditya Priyadarshin, or Ashok the Great, 321-270 BC.)
102 BC-15 AD	**Vikramaditya**, established the Vikram era in 57 BC.
(AD)	
25-85	**Shalivahan** (ruled for 60 years), established Shalivahan Shak era in 78 AD.
85-1192	There were several kingdoms of Rajpoot kings all over India. They ruled for 1,107 years.
1192-1757	In 1192, Mohammad Gori invaded Delhi (Hastinapur) the second time, defeated and killed Prithiviraj Chauhan, and became the king. Since then several dynasties of Muslims ruled India for 565 years, then,
1757-1947	In 1757, English regime was established in Bengal. British ruled India for 190 years.
1947	**India got Independence.**

Radha Krishn

CHAPTER TWO

Hinduism, a Divine manifestation.

(1) Actual age of the Vedas and the Puranas, the latest reproduction of the Vedas, Upnishads, grammar and the Puranas was about 5,000 years ago, personality of Ved Vyas, and prime theme of the Upnishads.*

We have the Vedas including the Upnishads, and also Upvedas, Vedangas and the Puranas, out of which the Upnishads and the Bhagwatam are the important ones. They were all produced by Brahma at the very beginning of the creation of this *brahmand*. Primarily they originated from God Vishnu Who is the Almighty aspect of supreme God Krishn. Then we have Smriti and Itihas. All of these scriptures were reproduced by Bhagwan Ved Vyas. We also have the Darshan Shastras, the Gita, writings of the *Jagadgurus* and other *acharyas* and Saints. These are our scriptures.

All the souls and the lifeless cosmic power *maya* are both eternal. (ज्ञाज्ञौ द्वावज... । क्षरं प्रधानम्... । श्वे. १/९,१०) Souls are under the

---

*The theme of all of the scriptures (Vedas, Upvedas, Vedangas, Kalp Sutras, Upnishads, all the Puranas, Gita, Bhagwatam, Ramayan and Mahabharat etc.) with Sanskrit quotations and the teachings and philosophies of all the Jagadgurus, *acharyas* and prominent Saints are described in the Part 2 of "The True History and the Religion of India."

influence and the bondage of *maya* since eternity. The Upnishads and the Puranas reveal the form of God and tell the procedure of freeing oneself from the bondage of *maya* with the Grace of God, and to realize the Divine Bliss. Now the question is: **when the bondage is eternal, its solution should also be eternally existing;** and the second thing is that every eternal existence has to be related to God and residing within God, because He is the supreme eternal Divine power.

The fact is, that the Vedas, Upnishads and the Puranas etc., *are* eternal; and they *are* eternal Divine powers residing in the abode of God Maha Vishnu. From Him they descend into the intellect of Brahma and then Brahma produces them in the world through the Sages. So, the Rigved (10/90/9), the Yajurved (31/7) and also the Atharvaved (19/6/13) authenticate the same truth, that all the Vedas were produced from God. The word is '*ajayat*' which means that they already existed in the Divine abode, God just produced them. (तस्माद्यज्ञात् सर्वहुत ऋचः सामानि जज्ञिरे। छन्दांसि जज्ञिरे तस्माद्यजुस्तस्मादजायत ॥)

The Brihadaranyak Upnishad says,

"ऋग्वेदो यजुर्वेदः सामवेदोऽथार्ङ्गिरसः इतिहासः पुराणं विद्या उपनिषदः श्लोकाः
सूत्राण्यनुव्याख्यानानिव्याख्यानान्यस्वैवैतानि निःश्वसितानि ॥"
(बृ. २/४/१०)

"Rigved, Yajurved, Samved, Atharvaved, Itihas (which is Ramayan and Mahabharat), Puran, Upvedas, Vedangas, Upnishads, (Sanskrit) language, and Sutras etc., were all produced by God."

The Bhagwatam says,

"ऋग्यजुःसामाथर्वाख्यान् वेदान् पूर्वादिभिर्मुखैः ॥
इतिहासपुराणानि पञ्चमं वेदमीश्वरः ।
सर्वेभ्य एव वक्त्रेभ्यः ससृजे सर्वदर्शनः ॥" (भा. ३/१२/३७, ३९)

"Brahma produced the eternal scriptures, Rigved, Yajurved, Samved, Atharvaved and also the Puranas which are like the fifth

Ved." He produced them at the very beginning of the creation of the world which was 155.52 trillion years ago.

Thus, the eternally existing Vedas and the Upnishads are the Divine knowledge itself. The Upnishads enlighten the souls with the knowledge of God. It leads to renunciation of worldly attachments and devotion (*bhakti*) to God, which, at the perfection (जुष्टं यदा पश्यति । मुं. ३/१/२) of total (रसं ्होवायं लब्ध्वाऽऽनन्दी भवति । तै. २/७) loving submission to God, reveals the Blissful form of God and the soul becomes Blissful forever. This is Ved, an eternal power of God.

So, now we know that the Vedas, the Upnishads and the Puranas are all eternal Divine knowledges which were given by God to Brahma and then Brahma produced them 155.52 trillion years ago to the Sages of this *brahmand,* who then produced them for the people of this earth planet, and Bhagwan Ved Vyas reproduced all of them before 3102 BC. Then why is it that these Indian and European writers unnecessarily tried to assume their date of production? It could be either to show off their intellectuality, or to release the prejudice of their heart, or to blindly follow earlier writers.

First take the examples of the writers like Jacobi or Tilak who said that the Rigved was written around 4500 or 4000 BC. They gave the reference of certain astrological indications which they found in the Rigved or some Grihya Sutra or Shatpath Brahman and produced their calculations. Every astrologer knows that the positions of the 27 *nakchatras* (lunar asterisms) in relation to the moon are always changing and that they are in a circular pattern. Thus, a particular position of the sun or a star or a *nakchatra* at a particular time and on a particular date of a year is such an event that would keep on repeating at the end of every cycle. It means the position of the stars which was on or about 4500 or 4000 BC, would have also been prior to that; and again prior to that also; and so on.

So it would also have been a million years ago or a billion years ago, or even trillions of years ago when the Sages of Bharatvarsh received the knowledge of the Vedas and Puranas from Brahma, because the astrological science of the movement of the *nakchatras* is always the same.

So one cannot claim on the basis of such astrological indications that the Rigved was written only in that particular period. According to their own speculative calculations writers have deduced various dates of Rigved from 2500 BC to about 9000 BC. However, we should know that the indications in the scriptures are not wrong, but interpretations of those people are wrong; and the most important thing is that **when the Vedas themselves are telling that they are eternal and are produced by God and it is an openly accepted fact that Bhagwan Ved Vyas himself reproduced all of them during the period of Krishn's descension,** why should one try to defy the Divine facts that are already established and show off a piece of his worldly intellectuality? It could only be out of his whim or ignorance, or the impurity of the mind, that restricts him from accepting the greatness of our Divine scriptures.

Jacobi was presumably ignorant about the Divine greatness of Bhartiya scriptures and Bhartiya civilization as he wrongfully wrote, "Punjab was the home of the earliest Vedic civilization," on page 91 of Ritambhara Studies in Indology, 1986 edition. Now coming to such writers who wrote that the Vedas were produced between 1000 and 1500 BC or maybe earlier; they were mostly the people who were associated with the Asiatic Society of Bengal. Their writings were motivated to demean the Vedic culture, so they simply poured the prejudice of their heart into their writings.

Thus we know that the Vedas with all of their affiliates, the Upnishads and the Puranas are all eternal.

✿✿✿

The latest reproduction of the Vedas, Upnishads, grammar and the Puranas about 5,000 years ago.

The Vedas have three sections: (1) *mantra* or *sanhita*, (2) *brahman* and (3) *aranyak*. *Mantras* are the invocative sentences related to the propitiation of the celestial gods to be used in the fire ceremonies (*yagya*) or for general prayer. There are also some parts in the *mantra* section that relate to supreme God (like the Purush Sookt of the Rigved (10/90) and the Ishopnishad, the 40th chapter of the Yajurved). *Brahman* section describes the details of the actual performance of the *yagyas*. Some part of it tells about the description of the worship of various almighty forms of God. *Aranyak* is like the final essence and the knowledge of the Vedas. It tells about God, His devotion and His supremacy. These are called the **Upnishads**. There are four Vedas: Rigved, Yajurved, Samved and Atharvaved. All the four have 1,180 branches. Accordingly there are 1,180 branches of the *brahman* section, and there are 1,180 Upnishads also. Only some branches of *mantra* and *brahman* section are available nowadays, but there are about 200 Upnishads which are still available.

As regards **Vedic grammar**, it was elaborated and expanded by quite a few Sages and Rishis and there was another book, the **Nirukt**, which explained the meaning of Vedic words. Later on Sage Panini wrote his grammar called Ashtadhyayi. It has a section called *unadi* which explains the formation of the words of Vedic *sanhita*. Panini, from a few sounds (like अइउण् ऋऌक् etc.) given by God Shiv, created the entire Sanskrit grammar. These are all Divine happenings on the material plane and are beyond the limits of material reasonings. **There is no one in the world who could create a perfect grammar from a few sounds, and this feature itself authenticates this fact that Sanskrit is a Divine manifestation on the material plane.**

Along with all the sections of the four Vedas, the Upvedas (the subsidiary Vedas: sociology, science of defense, music and medicine), and the Vedangas (affiliates of the Vedas), which include Sanskrit grammar, dictionary and astrology, were also revealed by Brahma to the Rishis in the very beginning. They were again reproduced by Ved Vyas about 5,000 years ago. He also produced the Mahabharat. He dictated and God Ganesh noted it down because it was a huge book and it needed a Divine mind to write it correctly. He also reproduced the Ramayan which was originally written by Sage Valmiki 18 million years ago during the descension period of Bhagwan Ram.

The aim of our scriptures is to guide a soul towards God realization. Thus, from a worldly person up to a highly evolved soul, they provide proper information for everyone and designate the form of devotion to God. It is a general axiom of the Divine world that any person of any class, kind or nature, if he selflessly surrenders to the supreme God with loving faith and determination, he receives His Grace; and, with His Grace, on the complete purification of the heart, the devotee receives God realization. To establish the greatness of loving devotion to God, called *bhakti*, Bhagwan Ram and Krishn descend on the earth planet from time to time. The pastimes of Bhagwan Ram and Krishn are described in the Ramayan and the Bhagwatam. Thus, we see that all of our scriptures from the Vedas up to the Bhagwatam are the Divine manifestations.

🟥🟥🟥

Personality of Ved Vyas.

Ved Vyas is one of the twenty-four descensions of God and every descension of God is absolute and eternal.

"सर्वे पुर्णाः शश्वताश्च देहास्तस्य परात्मनः ।"

However, in the practical life, most of them had a father and a mother who were Divine personalities. Accordingly, Ved Vyas was the son of Sage Parashar. He was born like a grown-up person and immediately he set out to the jungle. Soon after that he started revealing the scriptures. He lived during the time of King Shantanu, the grandfather of the Pandavas. Krishn Dwaipayan was his first name and Ved Vyas was his title because he revealed and systematized the *mantras* of the Vedas. He was also called Vadrayan because he lived for some time in the jungles of *vadari* (jungle of berries) in the Himalayas near Badrikashram. All of these names are famous in the scriptures, but for speaking convenience Ved Vyas or Bhagwan Ved Vyas is commonly used for him.

These are all Divine happenings. For your understanding you must know that Bhagwan Ved Vyas, who had conceived all of the scriptures in his Divine mind, systematically revealed them one after another. He revealed the Vedas including all 1,180 Upnishads and the affiliates and subsidiaries, 17 Puranas and 18 Uppuranas, the Mahabharat and the Ramayan, and at the end the Bhagwatam which is called the *Maha* Puran (the supreme Puran). Ved Vyas taught these scriptures to his God realized disciples who retained them in their Divine minds.

Prime theme of the Upnishads, Puranas, Gita and the Bhagwatam.

The Upnishads.

The Upnishads give two facts: (1) The first one is that soul does not belong to *maya* or the *mayic* world because it is itself an eternal, infinitesimal and Divine entity (ज्ञाज्ञौ द्वावजावीशनीशा... । श्वे. १/ ९), and (2) the second one is that the soul has a natural and eternal relationship with God. The Upnishads describe this fact with their aphorism तत्त्वमसि *tattvamasi* (छां. ६/८/७). It means: (a) (तत्सदृशं त्वम्) Soul (in its pure form) is substantially the same as God, like a drop of the ocean and the ocean itself. (b) (तस्य त्वम्) Soul belongs to God as it is eternally related to Him. Souls are unlimited in number. Thus, after knowing this fact, that you have all kinds of sweet relationships with God you have to love Him selflessly and wholeheartedly. (उपासते पुरुषं ये ह्यकामाः । मुं. ३/२/१, जुष्टं यदा पश्यति । मुं. ३/ १/२) This is called *bhakti* (selfless devotion to God) which is the true path to realize any form of God. The detailed account of *bhakti* and the description of the various self-submissive forms of one single God is in "Sanatan Dharm" and "The Divine Vision of Radha Krishn."

But, certain ignorant scholars and *sanyasis* who translated the Upnishads and wrote commentaries on them completely twisted their meaning and translated the word *brahm* as only 'formless and impersonal Divinity.'

In fact, in the Upnishads the term *brahm* refers mostly to the personal form of God. Out of 108 Upnishads there is only one verse (7) in the Mandukyopnishad that relates the actual form of *nirakar brahm.*

The Upnishads mostly use pronouns when referring to God, like, सः (He), ईशः (controller God), पुरुषः (personal God) and तस्य (His) etc.

In the Shvetashvatar Upnishad, over 40 times the personal form of God has been mentioned. For example: ईशः, देवम्, आत्मसंस्थम्, पुरुषम्, महान्तम्, सर्वव्यापी स भगवान्, प्रभुम्, शरणम्, धातः, सखाया, मायिनम्, वरदम्, ईड्यम्, भावग्राह्यम्, ईश्वराणां परमं महेश्वरम्, पतिं पतीनाम्, सर्वान्तरात्मा, इत्यादि । (श्वे.). They all relate to the Gracious personality of God Who is kind, the refuge of all the souls, master of *maya*, supreme controller of the universe, and the Soul of all the souls, etc. In the most famous verse of the Upnishad, "रसो वै सः ।"(*raso vai sah*), '*sah*' relates to the personal form of God and '*rasah*' relates to Krishn (Gopal Poorv Tapiniya Upnishad 2/13).

In this way the Upnishads, in their own style, describe the selfless devotion to God to receive His Grace and to be Blissful forever.

❀❀❀

The Puranas.

Puranas are large in number and each of them is in praise of a particular 'form' of God, such as, Shiv, Shakti, Vishnu, Ganesh etc. They are very attractive to materialists because they are full of stories of acquiring material riches and prosperity by devotion to that particular form of God described therein.

However, these stories do not aim at promoting selfish devotion, they simply give an attraction of the material gain so that one may decide to worship with that attraction; but, at the same time, it is clearly indicated that this worship must be sincere.

For instance: a mother develops a sense of greed in her son by saying, "If you go to school and learn your lessons properly, I will give you sweets." She knows the weakness of her child. She takes advantage of it and thus induces him in this manner to study his books. The mother's intention, in doing so, is not really to make him greedy, but to turn his mind to study rather than play. She knows that after having completed his elementary education, he himself will understand the importance of education and will naturally begin to love his studies.

In the same way, our Puranas do not teach that a person should become greedy, instead, they teach that one should enter into such a devotion which is always done with selfless love and surrender to God. They say, 'Love first, ask afterwards,' but we are so selfish that we never wish to love God, we simply go on making selfish demands from Him and still we think that we are the devotees of God. The fact is, that a person who wishes to make Him a means of material gains, is really a pure materialist.

Thus, it is clear that the expressions of 'material gain by devotion' are simply a '*simulating appearance*' of the *Puranas*. Their main object is to initiate a person into selfless devotion to God in His personal form.

The Gita.

Gita is the essence of all the Upnishads as it is spoken directly by Krishn.

When a person understands the importance of Divine attainment, Gita teaches him how to surrender to God while living in this world and facing worldly difficulties. The main theme of the Gita is revealed in the following verses which say that one should surrender one's intellect at the feet of Krishn, the absolute Divinity, and remember Him with faith and love, constantly and single-mindedly,

"योगिनामपि सर्वेषां मद्गतेनान्तरात्मना ।
श्रद्धावान्भजते यो मां स मे युक्ततमो मतः ॥ (गी. ६/४७)

अनन्यचेताः सततं यो मां स्मरति नित्यशः ।
तस्याहं सुलभः पार्थ नित्ययुक्तस्य योगिनः ॥ (गी. ८/१४)

मय्यावेश्य मनो ये मां नित्ययुक्ता उपासते ।
श्रद्धया परयोपेतास्ते मे युक्ततमा मताः ॥ (गी. १२/२)

मय्येव मन आधत्स्व मयि बुद्धिं निवेशय ।
निवसिष्यसि मय्येव अत ऊर्ध्वं न संशयः ॥ (गी. १२/८)

मन्मना भव मद्भक्तो मद्याजी मां नमस्करु ।
मामेवैष्यसि सत्यं ते प्रतिजाने प्रियोसि मे ॥" (गी. १८/६५)

Because: He is the supreme God and all other forms of God are established in Him;

"त्वमादिदेवः पुरुषः पुराणस्त्वमस्य विश्वस्य परं निधानम् ।" (गी. ११/३८)

He is the source and abode of absolute Truth, non differentiated *brahm* (*nirakar brahm*);

"ब्रह्मणो हि प्रतिष्ठाहममृतस्याव्ययस्य च ।" (गी. १४/२७)

He is the deliverer of liberation;

"तेषामहं समुद्धर्ता मृत्युसंसारसागरात् ।" (गी. १२/७)

He is the destination of all *Yogi*s and *Gyani*s; and,

"बहूनां जन्मनामन्ते ज्ञानवान्मां प्रपद्यते ।" (गी. ७/१९)

He is the master of material power (*maya*) which holds even the *gyanis* on the plane of ignorance.

"मयाध्यक्षेण प्रकृतिः सूयते सचराचरम् ।" (गी. ९/१०)

So, the Gita asserts that one should surrender to Krishn if one desires to get out of the cycle of *maya* and enter into His Divine abode.

❋❋❋

The Bhagwatam. Complete and Final Authority on the Divine Science.
(Taken from "The Science of Devotion and Grace")

Vallabhacharya has said in his writings,

"वेदाः श्रीकृष्णवाक्यानि, व्याससूत्राणि चैव हि ।
समाधिभाषा व्यासस्य, प्रमाणं तच्चतुष्टयम् ॥

उत्तरं पूर्वसन्देहवारकं परिकीर्तितम् ।
अविरुद्धं तु यत्त्वस्य प्रमाणं तच्च नान्यथा ।
एतद्विरुद्धं यत्सर्वं न तन्मानं कथंचन ॥" (निबन्ध ७, ८)

"There are four prime authoritative scriptures: the Ved, the Gita, the Brahm Sutra and the Bhagwatam. The latter ones are explanatory to the former ones. The Bhagwatam is the final authority, which, with its main philosophy of Divine love, contains all the philosophies of the Ved, the Brahm Sutra and the Gita. So, any spiritual principle or theory which appears to be disputing the theory of the Bhagwatam should not be considered as authentic."

As a rule, knowledge ends in love, so, where the philosophy of the Gita ends, the philosophy of the Bhagwatam begins. The Gita was spoken to Arjun when he was confused about the real aim of his life and was seeking Krishn's advice. Although he accepted Krishn as supreme God, he was not ready to fully surrender his intellect to Him. After a discourse of seven hundred verses, he was convinced and said to Krishn that he would follow His instructions without applying his own intellect as he had fully surrendered himself at His lotus feet.

So, the Gita mainly teaches about the surrender of the intellect and remembrance of Krishn with faith and love, and this can be seen throughout the whole book. For instance, see the verses 4/11, 7/19, 8/5, 8/14, 9/22, 9/29, 9/30, 9/34, 10/10, 10/65, 10/66, 11/54, 12/1, 12/2 and 12/8, etc.

If we study the Bhagwatam, we find that the entire philosophy of the Gita is described in its eleventh canto. Along with that, the main philosophy of the Bhagwatam relates to Divine love and its manifestations which are indicated in the Ved but are not explained in the Brahm Sutra or the Gita. The different manifestations of Divine love, their stages, their Blissful superiority and the marvel of Vrindaban Bliss above all other Blissful states of the Divine, are the subjects of practical experience which are beyond the imagination of even highly evolved souls. So, the philosophy of the Bhagwatam was imparted to a great Saint, Shukdeo, who had attained perfection and was fully absorbed in the deep ecstatic state of the Divine knowledge.

When Ved Vyas wrote the Bhagwatam he thought, "To whom should I impart this Divine secret?" He meditated and found that only his son Shukdeo was capable of retaining and understanding the knowledge of the Bhagwatam. So, he called for him through one of his pupils and taught him the Bhagwatam.

After listening to the virtues of Krishn, Shukdeo was so encharmed, that he forgot his *brahm gyan* forever and remembered only Radha.

Ved Vyas who edited the Vedas and wrote all of our scriptures, says,

"सर्ववेदान्तसारं हि श्रीभागवतमिष्यते ।
तद्रसामृततृप्तस्य नान्यत्र स्याद्रतिः क्वचित् ॥" (भा. १२/१३/१५)

"The essence of all kinds of *vedant* is imbued in the philosophy of the Bhagwatam. The one who has tasted the sweetness of its indicated form of 'Love' is contented forever, and he will never find any pleasure in indulging in the philosophy of other *isms*."

"निगमकल्पतरोर्गलितं फलं शुकमुखादमृतद्रवसंयुतम् ।
पिबत भागवतं रसमालयं मुहुर्होरसिका भुवि भावुकाः ॥" (भा. १/१/३)

"Bhagwatam is the luscious juice of that fully grown fruit which appeared on the tree of the Vedas and which is further enriched by the loving input of Shukdeoji. There is no waste matter in it, so this should be drunk continually by the *rasik* Saints and the devotees of Krishn forever."

The devotional theme of the Bhagwatam.

For the good of the souls Krishn has Himself revealed the secret of devotion to Uddhao.

Uddhao asks Krishn, "How can an ordinary person find the true path of God realization when every spiritual preacher in the world claims himself to be right?"

Krishn answers and says,

"मयाऽऽदौ ब्रह्मणे प्रोक्ता धर्मो यस्यां मदात्मक: ।
तेन प्रोक्ता च पुत्राय मनवे पूर्वजाय सा ।" (भा. ११/१४/३,४)

"I gave Vedic knowledge to Brahma in which the theme of My loving devotion and surrender was explained. That knowledge was transferred successively to other Saints."

"एवं प्रकृतिवैचित्र्याद् भिद्यन्ते मतयो नृणाम् ।
पारंपर्येण केषाञ्चित् पाखण्डमतयोऽपरे ॥

मन्मायामोहितधियः पुरुषाः पुरुषर्षभ ।
श्रेयो वदन्त्यनेकान्तं यथाकर्म यथारुचि ॥" (भा. ११/१४/८,९)

"When material beings tried to interpret the Ved, they explained it according to their own mentality and belief, as their minds were allured by the fascinating material power of *maya*. Thus, many fictitious paths of devotion and meditation came into being and were claimed to be Divine."

"धर्ममेके यशश्चान्ये कामं सत्यं शमं दमम् ।
अन्ये वदन्ति स्वार्थं वा ऐश्वर्यं त्यागभोजनम् ॥

केचिद् यज्ञतपोदानं व्रतानि नियमान् यमान् ।
आद्यन्तवन्त एवैषां लोकाः कर्मविनिर्मिताः ।
दुःखोदकांस्तमोनिष्ठाः क्षुद्रानंदाः शुचार्पिताः ॥" (भा. ११/१४/१०,११)

"Some talked about observing rituals and fastings; some talked about doing sacrifices and austerities; some talked about sensual restraint and renunciation; and some talked about doing good to others and not telling lies. But, in fact, all these good actions and practices simply lead to *mayic* darkness with better material enjoyments in the next life."

"न साधयति मां योगो न सांख्यं धर्म उद्धव ।
न स्वाध्यायस्तपस्त्यागो यथा भक्तिर्ममोर्जिता ॥

भक्त्याहमेकया ग्राह्यः श्रद्धयाऽऽत्मा प्रियः सताम् ।
भक्तिः पुनाति मन्निष्ठा श्वपाकानपि संभवात् ॥" (भा. ११/१४/२०,२१)

"Highly evolved *yog* and intellectually analyzed *gyan*, (knowledge), study of the *vedant* and the ascetic order of renunciation, religious and ritual observances (*dharm*), and penance and austerity, are uncertain ways of Divine attainment as compared to My devotional love. Only with faithful love and devotion can one find Me. There is no other way."

"यथाग्निः सुसमृद्धार्चिः करोत्येधांसि भस्मसात् ।
तथा मद्विषया भक्तिरुद्धवैनांसि कृत्स्नशः ॥

बाध्यमानोऽपि मद्भक्तो विषयैरजितेन्द्रियः ।
प्रायः प्रगल्भया भक्त्या विषयैर्नाभिभूयते ।" (भा. ११/१४/१९,१८)

"As the fire burns up a whole pile of logs, so, the flame of devotional love for Me burns up all the accumulated sins of the devotee. If My devotee, who has not conquered his sensual feelings, falls a victim to material allurements, he can easily overcome them because of his sincere faith and love for Me."

"निष्किञ्चना मय्यनुरक्तचेतसः शान्ता महान्तोऽखिलजीववत्सलाः ।
कामैरनालब्धधियो जुषन्ति यत् तन्नैरपेक्ष्यं न विदुः सुखं मम ॥" (भा. ११/१४/१७)

"My devotee Saints, who have attained Divine peace, who have affection for all the souls of the world, who have no ambition for worldly possessions and whose hearts are totally devoted to Me, worldly desires never touch their minds, because they have merged their own being in Me. The Divine pleasure of such Devotees is inexpressible."

"न पारमेष्ठ्यं न महेन्द्रधिष्ण्यं न सार्वभौमं न रसाधिपत्यम् ।
न योगसिद्धीरपुनर्भवं वा मय्यर्पितात्मेच्छति मद्विनान्यत् ॥

न तथा मे प्रियतम आत्मयोनिर्न शङ्करः ।
न च सङ्कर्षणो न श्रीर्नैवात्मा च यथा भवान् ॥

निरपेक्षं मुनिं शान्तं निर्वैरं समदर्शनम् ।
अनुव्रजाम्यहं नित्यं पूयेयेत्यङ्घ्रिरेणुभिः ॥" (भा. ११/१४/१४,१५,१६)

"My Devotees never wish for the highest riches, not even the throne of Brahma and Indra or the sovereignty of the world. The highest powers (*siddhis*) of *yog* and the absolute emancipation are nothing for them, because they have merged their heart and soul in Me. They wish only to serve Me and they desire only to love Me.

Truly speaking, such Saints are more loving to Me than My own emanations (*swansh*), such as, Shiv, Maha Lakchmi and My brother Balram. What more remains to be said, I always follow them to Grace Myself with their foot dust."

"धर्मः सत्यदयोपेतो विद्या वा तपसान्विता ।
मद्भक्त्याघ्यापेतमात्मानं न सम्यक् प्रपुनाति हि ॥" (भा. ११/१४/२२)

"Truthfully and compassionately observed *dharm* (rituals and social good deeds) and austerely attained knowledge (*gyan*) are incapable of purifying the heart fully, unless they are predominated with My *bhakti*."

"यथाग्निना हेम मलं जहाति ध्मातं पुनः स्वं भजते च रूपम् ।
आत्मा च कर्मानुशयं विधूय मद्भक्तियोगेन भजत्यथो माम् ॥" (भा. ११/१४/२५)

"Unless the heart of a devotee is melted by the feeling of My loving separation, tears of love will not come, and without the tears of selfless love, how can a devotee's heart be purified? When an impure piece of gold is put into a powerful fire, it adopts the qualities of the fire. Foreign elements leave it and it becomes pure. In the same way, when the flame of devotional love bursts forth in the heart of a devotee, it burns up the sins, cleans it, and, on the complete purification, he attains Me."

"यथा यथाऽऽत्मा परिमृज्यतेऽसौ मत्पुण्यगाथाश्रवणाभिधानैः ।
तथा तथा पश्यति वस्तु सूक्ष्मं चक्षुर्यथैवाञ्जनसम्प्रयुक्तम् ॥" (भा. ११/१४/२६)

"As the heart of My devotee is purified by the listening and chanting of My virtues and plays, he gradually receives the devotional experiences of My love and Divine secrets are gradually revealed to him. Just as, when a person applies an infallible medicine to his sick eyes, his vision gradually improves and the grandeur of beauty and color is slowly revealed to him."

This verse explains the feelings and the external indications of a *rasik* Saint who has attained Divine love. Krishn says,

"वाग् गद्गदा द्रवते यस्य चित्तं रुदत्यभीक्ष्णं हसति क्वचिच्च ।
विलज्ज उद्गायति नृत्यते च मद्भक्तियुक्तो भुवनं पुनाति ॥" (भा. ११/१४/२४)

"My loving Devotee (the *rasik* Saint) whose heart is always filled with My love, when he chants the Divine name or sings the songs of My *leelas* or virtues, the tone of his voice changes due to Divine excitement and his heart melts. He feels the intensity of My love and enters into *Bhao*. (*Bhao* is the ecstatic state of Divine love which arises in his heart in the form of dual emotional feelings of meeting and separation.) In *Bhao*, he yearns and cries to get My vision and laughs in happiness when he receives it. (These ecstatic expressions are called *sattvic bhao* or the Divine expressions.) His feeling of love deepens and He feels My close personal association. In this excitement, He rises and sings and dances in *Bhao*. Such a *rasik* Saint, who is ever absorbed in My Love, purifies the world with his Divine-love-consciousness and gratifies the surroundings with his presence."

Krishn further gives some instructions to the devotees, He says,

"न तथास्य भवेत् क्लेशो बन्धश्चान्यप्रसङ्गतः ।
योषित्सङ्गाद् यथा पुंसो यथा तत्सङ्गसङ्गिनः ॥" (भा. ११/१४/३०)

"An intelligent devotee must keep himself detached from the association of the opposite sex and sensualists, because the attachments and sufferings born of such associations are greater as compared to other material associations."

"विषयान् ध्यायतश्चित्तं विषयेषु विषज्जते ।
मामनुस्मरतश्चित्तं मय्येव प्रविलीयते ॥

तस्मादसदभिध्यानं यथा स्वप्नमनोरथम् ।
हित्वा मयि समाधत्स्व मनो मद्भावभावितम् ॥

स्त्रीणां स्त्रीसङ्गिनां सङ्गं त्यक्त्वा दूरत आत्मवान् ।
क्षेमे विविक्त आसीनश्चिन्तयेन्मामतन्द्रितः ॥" (भा. ११/१४/२७,२८,२९)

"When a person is desirous of sensual objects and their enjoyments, his mind gets more and more attached to them; but if he faithfully remembers Me, his mind gets more and more absorbed in My love. So, he should leave the daydreaming of attaining the illusive pleasures of the material objects and try to engross his mind in Me with a steady consciousness of My love. Keeping himself aloof from sensual associations and thoughts, a person should choose a solitary place where he should selflessly remember Me with deep affinity."

The above is the translation of the original text. Going through it, one can understand that without true *bhakti* no one can enter the Divine abode. All other ways of *yog*, *gyan*, *austerity* and *meditation* remain only as supplementary to *bhakti*. They can never be the independent ways of God realization. Only *bhakti* (divine-love-devotion) is the independent and direct approach to supreme Divinity, Krishn, Whose Divine love is so charming and sweet that it supercedes the excellence of the Divine Bliss of all the Divine abodes.

A *rasik* Saint says,

"जे अवतार कदम्ब भजत हैं धरि दृढ़ ब्रत जु हिये ।
तेऊ तजति उमगि मर्यादा बन बिहार रस पिये ॥"

"The charm of Krishn's beauty is so great and the sweetness of Krishn's love is so excellent, that whosoever tastes the nectar of Krishn love, abandons his previous worship of other form of God (such as Vishnu, Shiv etc.) and drowns himself in the supreme Divine Bliss of Krishn *leelas*."

(2) Bhartiya scriptures are Divine manifestations.

Bhartiya scriptures are very specific. They themselves tell who is qualified to study them and when were they produced. For example: The very first line of the Brahm Sutra says that only an extremely renounced true aspirant of God is qualified to study it and the Bhagwatam tells that anyone who has a deep and sincere desire to receive the Divine love of God can study it. *These Divine scriptures* (the Vedas, Upnishads, Puranas, Gita and the Bhagwatam etc.) teach the path to God so they are never meant for the atheists, and moreover a nonbeliever in the Divinity of Hindu scriptures can never understand their true theme by merely learning the Sanskrit language* (see p. 21).

The Upnishads, which are the most important sections of the Vedas, themselves mention their eternity, as being a Divine power of God. The Brihadaranyakopnishad (2/4/10) says that the Rigved, Yajurved, Samved, Atharvaved, history books (like Ramayan and Mahabharat), all the Puranas (including the Bhagwatam), the Upnishads and the Sanskrit language with its vocabulary (and grammar) are all produced by the supreme God (on the earth planet through the creator Brahma).

The Sages and Saints whose names appear in the Upnishads and the Puranas are eternal Saints who descend on the earth planet

---

*Bhartiya religion (**Sanatan Dharm**) and its scriptures are eternal and Divine. Apart from it there are eleven prime religions in the world that were produced sometime within 4,000 years by an individual or a group of people. They are: Buddhism and Jainism (non-Godly religions); Sikhism (devotion to impersonal God); Zoroastrianism (fire-god worshippers); two Muslim religions; Jewish and Christian religions (referring to unidentified god and the god of heaven); Shintoism of Japan (worshipers of nature spirits); and Confusianism and Taoism of China (the first one deals with social morals of a man and the second one is more towards evolution of the self through meditation and self discipline).

to reveal the Divine knowledge. The teachings of the Upnishads are in the form of questions and answers. Just like, the questions and the answers of Sages Shaunak and Angira became the Mundakopnishad, and the conversation between Sage Yagyavalkya, King Janak and others became a major part of the Shvetashvataropnishad. The conversation between the Sages of Brahm lok and the creator Brahma, who is the original knower of the Vedas and Puranas, is the Gopal Poorb Tapiniyopnishad.

In the scriptures there are quite a good number of repetitions. The same theory of renunciation from the attachments, illusion of *mayic* happiness, Divineness of the souls, and the supremacy of God's Bliss are repeatedly described in various ways in the Upnishads; and, in the Puranas, similar stories of devotion, God's Grace and His acts etc., have been liberally repeated. Also all of the Divine truth is not described at one place or in one volume of writing.

Sometimes these writings appear to be contradictory, but in fact they are not. For a Divine personality there is no contradiction at all, because he sees the reality. It is only the material mind, because of its little-knowingness, that sees some discrepancies in certain descriptions.

You should know that scriptural knowledge is only for the practice of God realization and not for intellectual speculation. It is forewarned at many places in the Upnishads that only through a God realized Saint, the real truth of the scriptures could be learned. So it is cautioned that, (श्रवणं तु गुरोः पूर्वकम्) a seeker of God's love and vision should learn the scriptures from such a learned Saint who knows the intricacies of scriptural writings.

❀❀❀

Divine writings cannot be analyzed in a material way.

It's a common universal rule that a layman cannot argue with the opinion of an expert although both are in the material field.

Then how could a worldly being, possessed with the vehemence of his own passions and desires, try to argue with the writings of Sages and Saints whose entire life was a Divine benevolence for the souls of the world? But it is seen that in the last few centuries most of the European writers, for some of their own personal reasons, willfully tried to derogate our religion and culture to the limits of their egotism, and a number of our Hindu writers followed the same trend.

You must know that the outcome of a material mind is always imperfect no matter how much of a genius a person is. But the Divine writings of our Divine personalities are always perfect and complete. As far as the historic part of our scriptures is concerned it is just the actual happening which is described in it. But the descriptions of our Puranas, Upnishads and the other scriptures are not only the happenings of the material plane, they also include the happenings of the Divine and the celestial dimensions. This is the reason that sometimes they don't fit within the conceptual framework of a material mind.

So, one has to expand the mental vision of his understanding to comprehend the truth of those happenings. But, it happened that the subtle effects of the diplomatically pre-planned derogative writings on Hindu culture and religion by the Europeans like Sir William Jones and Max Müller etc. infected the minds of certain Hindu intellectuals to such an extent that, forgetting our Divine greatness, they also started calling our Puranas a myth which is an absolutely misleading term. It is like someone announcing that he himself is dead. If he is dead, how could he announce about his death. It could only be an expression of the instability of his mind. **You should know that all of our religious writings are Divine facts, and facts always remain the facts.** *Disregarding their Divine greatness and using the word myth for our religious history is a serious spiritual transgression.*

Documentary evidences show that Brahma, creator of our *brahmand*, received the Divine knowledge of all the scriptures along with the Sanskrit language from the supreme God Krishn. Brahma revealed the same knowledge (155 trillion years ago) to the Rishis of the earth planet who then revealed it to the souls of the world.

(3) Evidences of the Divine authenticity of Bhartiya scriptures.

There are three kinds of evidences: documentary, inferential and perceptional. In the scriptural terms they are called *shabd* (documentary), *anuman* (inferential or circumstantial) and *pratyakch* (perceptional). We have all the three kinds of evidences to authenticate the Divinity of all the scriptures along with their descriptions.

(a) We have a system. The scriptures themselves tell their origin in their writings. The Upnishads, which are the first revelations, tell that the Vedas, the Upnishads and all of the Rishis and Sages were produced by God Maha Vishnu Himself and are protected by Him.

"सर्वे ऋषयः सर्वाणिछन्दसि नारायणादेव समुत्पद्यन्ते । नारायणात्प्रवर्तन्ते ॥"
(त्रि. महा.)

Not only at one place but at many places it has been documented in the Upnishads. The Brihadaranyakopnishad (2/4/10) says that all the four Vedas, Upnishads, Puranas, History and other affiliates and subsidiaries of the Vedas along with their grammar were produced by God Himself. Again, in the Chandogyopnishad (7/1/2) it is said that the History (called Itihas, which are: the Ramayan and the Mahabharat) and Puranas are like the fifth Ved. Also, regarding the period of their reproduction by Ved Vyas and the time of the war, the Mahabharat gives the precise astronomical data when the war had happened.

(b) Considering the depth, extensiveness, preciseness and perfection of such scriptural knowledges that are beyond human intellect, it can easily be inferred that it is super-material knowledge, thus it can only be Divine. The depth of the philosophy of God and God realization with its detailed descriptions, the extensiveness of the historical descriptions in the Puranas and in the Mahabharat, the preciseness of the calculations of the periods and the cycles of 'time' (for example: the beginning of the existing human civilization is 120.5331 million years; the age of the earth planet and also the existing form of the sun is 1971.9616 million years in 1998; the very beginning of this planetary system is 155.521972 trillion years), and the perfection of the Sanskrit grammar since it was introduced on the earth planet through the early Sages of India, are all such unequalled examples which naturally certify the Divine greatness of our scriptures.

(c) As regards perception of the Divine, every God realized *bhakt* Saint all the time witnesses the Divine glory of his beloved God and, remaining in His association, conceives the theme of all the scriptures. That's how when he writes anything it is perfectly in coordination with the tenets of the original scriptures. There are an enormous number of such examples. As far as the existence of the celestial abodes and its gods are concerned we don't need a true Saint to certify it, even an evolved *yogi* who has perfected his *samadhi* could visualize the celestial gods during the meditative part of his *samadhi*.

From the very recent to the very ancient time we have such biographies of the *rasik* Saints whose Divine association with Krishn is generously described. There were a great number of Saints in Braj in the last 500 years who wrote about their visualization of the playfulness of Krishn in the form of songs called *pad*. They are in thousands and are all printed in book form. A *rasik* Saint, Surdas, is said to have sung more than a hundred thousand songs about the playfulness of the supreme God Krishn. It means that he sang at least 15 to 25 songs every day. Out of them more than two thousand songs are still available. It was the beauty of his description that he sang them simultaneously as he visualized them. These Saints also wrote the philosophical aspects of the form and the virtues of God and the true path of God realization. **In this way they witnessed the Divinity and authenticated the Divineness of our scriptures.**

We have thus abundance of evidences of all kinds that authenticate the eternal Divineness and the greatness of our scriptures, the Vedas, the Upnishads, the Puranas, the Mahabharat and the Ramayan etc., which delineate the Divine history of Sages, Saints, Divine personalities and the descensions of the supreme God. They also describe the simple and the easy path of God realization through devotion (*bhakti*) and dedication while detailing the philosophical aspects of the Divine dimensions and the forms of God.

Classifications of Bhartiya scriptures.

In a city there are kindergarten schools, elementary schools, high schools, colleges and maybe a university. From the kindergarten and up to the university, all the institutions are called the educational institutions and their aim is to remove illiteracy and make a person educated, but all of them are not for all the people of that town. They have classifications according to merit as to who could be admitted to which institution and in which grade or in which kind of study.

Similarly, all of our scriptures are collectively called "Sanatan Dharm" which means the eternal (*sanatan*) knowledge for the spiritual well being of all the souls (*dharm*). It provides the guidelines for all kinds of people of the world, which, if followed, leads them towards God realization. But the scriptures of Sanatan Dharm, like the various educational institutions of a town, are specified according to a person's receptivity for God as to which scripture one should follow.

The Vedas: For example: A wicked person should at least think of God that He knows everything, so He will punish him for his wicked deeds. A selfish and worldly person should at least follow the disciplines of the **Vedas** and do good deeds and learn to pray to any form of God or he may do any ritualistic *yagya* even with a worldly desire to obtain the celestial luxury.

The technical requirements of doing a *yagya* are hard to fulfill in *kaliyug*. Thus, the Sages have promulgated that **the Vedic *yagyas* are not suitable for *kaliyug*,** and so, only the good deeds, prayer and honest behavior as mentioned above should be observed by those kind of people in this age.

The other good actions which are also involved in the performance of the *yagyas* are: giving charity, maintaining piousness and celibacy during the period of doing *yagya*, and praying to God for the purification of the mind; and afterwards he is supposed to observe honest behavior in his life. These good actions slowly purify the heart of the doer, and thus, he could become qualified to enter into direct devotion to one form of God which is like taking an admission into high school from an elementary school.

The Upnishads: When a person begins to feel a real liking for God but still he is attached to his material enjoyments and he keeps on doing good deeds, the **Upnishads** help him at this stage and tell him about the futility of worldly pleasures and advise him to renounce worldly attachments and wholeheartedly love God.

The Gita: When the person enters into such a stage of heart purification where he really begins to realize the worthlessness of worldly pleasures and feels an urge to meet God, the **Gita** tells that the secret of devotion to God is selfless *bhakti*. It means selflessly loving Krishn and living in the world to fulfill your aim of God realization. Selflessness means not desiring any worldly thing from God but desiring only for His love and vision. You should know that the *nirakar brahm* along with the other forms of God (God Vishnu, God Shiv and Goddess Durga etc.) are established in the personality of Krishn.

The Bhagwatam: When a devotee has understood the importance of pure and selfless *bhakti,* then the **Bhagwatam** tells the devotee that the sweetest and the real intimate form of God is Krishn Whose soul is Radha. Thus, Both Radha and Krishn are one. Their bewitching beauty had enchanted everyone who was living in Braj at that time.

When a devotee is fallen in love with Krishn then the writings of the *rasik* Saints tell more about the *leelas* of Radha Krishn and the richness of the Blissful stages of Divine love which are experienced in Golok and in Divine Vrindaban.

Thus, the Vedas tell to become a good person; Upnishads tell to love God and don't be attached in the world because it is illusion; the Gita tells to love God selflessly and reveals the secret of the spiritual practices that *only through bhakti* one can realize God; and then the Bhagwatam tells what is the most loving form of God that encharmed the heart of God Shiv and the topmost *Yogi* and *Gyani,* Shukdeo.

Now, we know that our scriptures are a very systematic line of teachings. They relate to every class of people of the world from an ordinary worldly person to a highly evolved soul deeply longing to meet God. But, every scripture is not for everyone; just like a book, prescribed for postgraduate classes, is no good for the student of a lower grade, and vice versa. However, as a whole, all the scriptures represent such Divine teachings which accommodate the spiritual need of all the souls of the world and show the path of God realization. **This is Sanatan Dharm or the Hindu religion which is the "universal religion" for the whole world that originated directly from the supreme God.** It was first introduced by Brahma to the Sages and Saints of this *brahmand* who produced it for the people of the earth planet. Lastly it was again reproduced by Bhagwan Ved Vyas about 5,000 years ago and its Divineness was further magnified in the celebrated writings of our great *acharyas.*

A devotee having the vision of God Shiv.

A devotee having the vision of Goddess Durga.

(4) The references and the stories of the Upnishads and the Puranas are supernatural happenings.

Divine acts and the Divine happenings are beyond material logic. There is no room for quibbling 'whys' and 'hows' over there. They could be understood with a pure heart and a sincere mind, willing to understand and accept the truth of devotion to God.

All the happenings that are described in the Upnishads or the Puranas are real and historical happenings. It is true that they may not be fully intelligible to a material mind but no part of them is unreal or imaginary. **They are the true history of the entire brahmand, not only of this earth planet,** and they are meant for the material souls of the world to show them the futility of the *mayic* manifestations, the Divine greatness of the Sages and Saints, and the path of *bhakti.*

The material reasonings are conditioned to, and based upon, the limitations of material time and space, and the spot-existency of an event. This is the reason that the happenings, that are beyond the *mayic* sphere, cannot be intellectualized.

There are three dimensions (material, celestial and Divine) and two kinds of space (material and celestial) in this *brahmand.*

Brahmand means the material and the celestial creation of one single Brahma. Material creation consists of an earth planet with a sun, moon and planetary system in the material space; and in the celestial space, which is just next to it, there is a celestial creation.

The topmost celestial abode called Brahm lok belongs to the creator Brahma, and adjacent to it are the abodes of God Shiv,

Goddess Durga and God Vishnu. The abodes of Vishnu, Shiv and Durga **represent a branch of Vaikunth abode in the celestial space of this brahmand.**

Brahma with other celestial gods like, Indra (king of the celestial abode and also god of rain, thunder and lightning), Vayu (god of air), Agni (god of fire), Varun (god of water), Kuber (god of wealth), Brihaspati (god of wisdom) and Prajapati (president of the gods' kingdom) etc. **represent the celestial creation. Material and celestial creations are the two (material and celestial) dimensions of the material power maya.**

The Divine dimension is equally omnipresent in both of the *mayic* dimensions. It includes all of the Divine forms and abodes of God, but it is invisible to *mayic* souls and also to the celestial beings.

The events described in our Upnishads and the Puranas are of seven kinds.

1. Happenings of the celestial abode in the celestial dimension. They are like the stories of war between demons and gods, or a certain demon terrorizing the celestial abode, and also its related stories. The ocean churning event, or such stories and events that involve Brahma, Indra, Rishis, Sage Narad, God Shiv and God Vishnu etc.

2. Happenings of the celestial abode involving the Divine dimension. Just like the description of Krishn's descension in the Garg Sanhita when God Vishnu, Brahma and other gods went to Golok to seek the favor of Krishn to descend to the earth planet to kill the demon Kans.

3. Happenings of the earth planet reflecting the Divine dimension. They are mostly related to Bhagwan Ram and Krishn. Just like: When Bhagwan Ram came to Ayodhya after conquering Lanka, He saw the loving impatience of His family members and the people of Ayodhya so He multiplied Himself into innumerable forms and instantly met everyone, and such was the beauty of this Gracious act that everyone felt that Ram came to him first.

"अमित रूप प्रगटे तेहि काला । जथा जोग मिले सबहिं कृपाला ॥"

In the Govardhan *leela,* Krishn playfully lifted the hill on His little finger and under the hill there was enough space to accommodate all the *Brajwasis* so they could stay there and spend the night. It all happened in a flash.

4. Happenings of the earth planet in the Divine dimension. The most important (*leela*) of this kind is *maharas* when unlimited *Gopis* danced with Krishn on the soils of Vrindaban but in a Divine dimension. A number of *nikunj leelas* and the *leelas* of Gahvarban were also the *leelas* of the Divine dimension where only *Gopis* and Radha Krishn associated.

5. Happenings of the earth planet mixed with the celestial dimension. (a) A good example of such a happening is the story of Nachiketa of Kathopnishad when he went to the celestial god Yam, asked spiritual questions, conceived the Divine truth, and crossed the *mayic* realm of death and birth. (b) According to the Ramayan, King Dashrath sometimes visited god Indra and accepted his hospitality. (c) The stories of Mahabharat when Arjun, during his exile period, visited celestial abodes and obtained celestial weapons from god Indra and Shiv etc., are of the same category. (d) Narad and God Shiv etc., visiting Braj and enjoying Krishn *leelas* are also of the same category.

6. Happenings of the earth planet that are beyond the logic and the limitations of the material phenomena. Lots of stories of our scriptures and the Puranas come in this category that are related to certain individual Saints, Sages and Rishis. For example: (a) Shukdeo remained for twelve years in the womb of his mother without giving her any discomfort. On the request of his father, Ved Vyas, when he came out, he was of the age and the height of a twelve year old boy. Not only that, he was fully absorbed in the

Bliss of *nirakar brahm*; he didn't even look to anyone around him. He just walked straight into the jungle. (b) To continue the family succession of a royal dynasty that had no heir, Ved Vyas simply looked to the two queens from a distance and they conceived. They gave birth to Pandu (the father of the Pandavas) and Dhritrashtra (the father of the Kauravas). (c) King Drupad was conducting a *yagya.* From the fire of the *yagya* a girl appeared and she was Dropadi, who married the Pandavas. Such happenings are beyond *mayic* nature, so they cannot be judged according to the material reasonings because they are promoted with the Divine power of a Divine personality.

7. **Normal happenings of this world as described in the Puranas etc.** All the happenings that are related to a person's day to day life are of this kind. In this world there are always *mayic* souls and some Saints. Sometimes certain eternal Divine personalities descend in the world, and there is a time when Bhagwan Ram and Krishn also descend on this earth planet. It's all described in the Puranas. **These happenings are of two kinds: material and Divine. All the actions of a mayic soul are material, and all the actions of the Divine personalities are Divine.**

Thus, the stories of the Puranas are repeated in a somewhat similar style. Details may differ but the general story remains almost the same. For example: the twelfth canto of the Bhagwatam predicts the detailed descriptions of the kings of India for about three thousand years. Suppose, after millions of years Krishn again descends on the earth planet and the Bhagwatam is again written by a Divine personality, Ved Vyas, of that time. There may not be a similar description of the dynasties of the kings of *kaliyug* as it is described in the twelfth canto, or there may be some variation in the descriptions of the first nine cantos, but the main part of the Krishn *leelas*, like the Govardhan *leela,* Brahma's confusion, saving the people of Braj from the demons of Kans, His loving childhood *leelas, maharas,* Mathura and Dwarika *leela,* the Mahabharat war and the teachings of the Gita will all be there. It means that the general characteristical body of the events with its special representation of Divine love and Divine knowledge that forms the main body of the Bhagwatam never changes. It remains the same forever, because the Bhagwatam is a Divine power of Golok abode.

Now we understand that the stories and the events that are described in the Upnishads and the Puranas are not only the material happenings just like the other historical events of the world, they are mostly the Divine happenings that involved all the three dimensions: material, celestial and the Divine. If we hold such a wide angle of view, keeping in mind the various dimensions and the classes and the kinds of the happenings of this *brahmand*, of which this earth planet is only a part, there remains no question, confusion or contradiction in a person's mind; and he begins to admire the Graciousness of God Who Himself revealed His knowledge to us. We should know that the stories of the Puranas explain the futility of worldly pleasures and teach the path of *bhakti* for every soul of the world.

Ancient scriptures:
Narad Bhakti Sutra, Shandilya Bhakti Sutra

CHAPTER THREE

Timeless uniqueness of the Sanskrit language.

(1) The Divine language of Bhartiya scriptures.

The Divineness of Sanskrit language is self-evident. You don't light up a candle to see the sun; just open your eyes and see it. But if you deliberately shut your eyes then how could you see the sun. Scriptures themselves tell about the eternal Divineness of the Sanskrit language and thousands of learned Saints and *acharyas* have already proclaimed its Divine authenticity. The first introductory verse of the Panini grammar tells that it came from God Shiv. Moreover, if you look from the **historical and logical point of view**, you will find that since the very first day the linguists have learned about the existence of the Sanskrit language, they have seen it in the same perfect form. *No sound shift, no change* in the vowel system, and *no addition* was ever made in the grammar of the Sanskrit in relation to the formation of the words. It is in its totally perfect form since it landed on the earth planet with its 52 letter alphabet. As regards its vocabulary, it had abundance of words and its grammar had a capacity of creating any number of new words for a new situation or concept or thing, and the same we have up till today. **Its alphabet, vowels and the exacting nature**

of the pronunciation of the letters and words were all perfect and the same since the very beginning.

There is no other example of the same kind in the world; and, in the last 5,000 years, since the Sumerians twittered the communicating words in a very limited scope and their wedge-shaped cuneiform writing came into existence, there was no such genius born who could produce a grammar as perfect as Sanskrit. Whereas all the languages of the world started from scratch with incomplete alphabet and vowels, not altogether of their own, borrowed from others to improve it, had only a few words in the beginning which were just enough for the people to communicate with each other, and it took a very long time to establish a proper literary form of that language. Even the advanced international language of today, **the English language**, when it took its roots from the West Germanic around 800 AD, it was in an absolutely primitive form. As it developed, it assimilated about 30% of its words from Latin and a lot of words from French and Greek. Slowly developing and improving its vocabulary, the style of writing and the grammar, from Old English (which had only two tenses) to Middle English, to Early Modern English, and then to Modern English, it took a very long time. As late as the beginning of the seventeenth century when its *first dictionary* was published in London in **1604** it had only 3,000 words, and the title of the dictionary was, **"A Table Alphabetical, conteyning and teaching the true writing and understanding of hard unusual English wordes, borrowed from the Hebrew, Greeke, Latine or French & c."** Somewhat similar is the story of all the ancient and modern languages when they started from a very primitive stage of their literal representation with no regular grammar, because the proper grammar was introduced at a much later date when they reached to a significant level of communication.

If you look to the history of the languages of the world you will find that they went through a number of stages of their development. **But the Sanskrit language was absolutely perfect by all means from the very beginning. Is it not enough evidence** to understand that it is not man-made and it is a Divine gift?

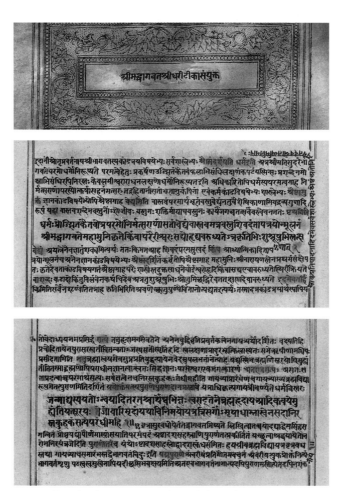

Handwriten manuscript of the Bhagwatam.

Major languages of the European family.
The most important language family of today.

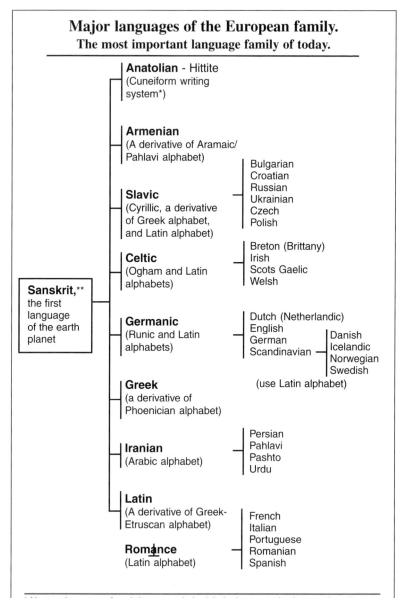

Anatolian - Hittite
(Cuneiform writing system*)

Armenian
(A derivative of Aramaic/ Pahlavi alphabet)

Slavic
(Cyrillic, a derivative of Greek alphabet, and Latin alphabet)

Bulgarian
Croatian
Russian
Ukrainian
Czech
Polish

Celtic
(Ogham and Latin alphabets)

Breton (Brittany)
Irish
Scots Gaelic
Welsh

Sanskrit, ** the first language of the earth planet

Germanic
(Runic and Latin alphabets)

Dutch (Netherlandic)
English
German
Scandinavian —

Danish
Icelandic
Norwegian
Swedish

(use Latin alphabet)

Greek
(a derivative of Phoenician alphabet)

Iranian
(Arabic alphabet)

Persian
Pahlavi
Pashto
Urdu

Latin
(A derivative of Greek-Etruscan alphabet)

Romance
(Latin alphabet)

French
Italian
Portuguese
Romanian
Spanish

* Next to the name of each language their alphabetic system is also mentioned.
** **Indian languages:** Hindi, Bengali, Gujarati, Marathi and South Indian languages are the descendants of Sanskrit language. Sindhi and Punjabi are the derivatives of Hindi and Urdu languages.

(2) Eternal perfection of the Sanskrit language and the other languages of the world.

We have already explained about the perfection and the eternal stability of the Sanskrit language. Anyone studying Sanskrit grammar understands these facts from the beginning as they are the basic characteristics of the Sanskrit language, whereas all the western and the Middle East writing systems developed from the Phoenician and Aramaic alphabets which only had syllabic consonants and no vowels, and that also in an incomplete form.

Major languages of the European family.
The most important language family of today.

An image of the alphabet and vowel system and certain *apbhranshas* of the Sanskrit language are found in every language of the world because Sanskrit is the first language of the earth planet. Its *apbhranshas* are seen more in the languages of the European family because these countries had more frequent trade connections with India, and thus, the people of these countries also had social connections with India to some extent. That's why Pahlavi of Persia had lots of Sanskrit *apbhransh* words in it. (See diagram facing page.)

Languages of the world.

These languages never had their own alphabet. The Iranian language, Persian, borrowed its alphabet three times from three different sources (cuneiform to Aramaic to Arabic) within 1,300 years and in its advanced stage it has only three (a, i, u) vowel marks which are used for both long and short sounds. They are totally inadequate to give the correct pronunciation of the words. So, unless you know the words, you cannot pronounce them correctly. The Greek language started from incomplete consonants which was borrowed from Northern (Phoenician) Semites, then added some vowels, improved the shape of the letters, added more long and short vowels, and thus, improved the language by constantly changing, altering, adding and modifying the word morphology, their inflection and the syntax as well. It also improved its vocabulary by borrowing the words from other languages, and thus, bringing it to the level of its modern standard where still a number of grammatical imperfections exist. Similar is the history of all the languages of the world. Latin and English languages also went through a number of changes before even their vocabulary was standardized from Germanic tribal language, which adopted Latin alphabet and then modified it.

Now we will give you a detailed explanation about the eternal Divinity of Sanskrit language.

Brahma revealing the Divine knowledge along
with the Sanskrit language to the Rishis.

(3) The six unmatched features of the Sanskrit language.

1. The vowel-consonant pronunciation of the alphabet.

The most striking feature of the Sanskrit language is the vowel-consonant pronunciation of the alphabet and the uniqueness of every consonant (or its combination) as a complete syllabic unit when it is joined with a vowel. For example: Its 16 vowels are the actual 'voice pattern' of the sound and 36 consonants are only the 'form' of the 'voice pattern' of the sound. So a consonant (क्,ख्,ग्) alone cannot be pronounced as it is only a 'form' of the 'voice pattern' until it is attached to a vowel. Thus, a vowel, which itself is a 'voice pattern,' can be pronounced (like, अ = a, ओ = o) alone or it can be modulated by adding a consonant to it (like, क् + अ = ka, ख्+ आ = kha, क् + ओ = ko).

This system was not adopted in the languages of the world. Thus, their syllables have no uniformity, like in *come* and *coma* where 'co' has two different pronunciations, and in *come* and *kind* or *kiss*, the letter 'c' and 'k' both have the same pronunciation.

The Greeks adopted five vowels from the Sanskrit literature, and some of the daily usable *apbhransh* words and numerals, like *trya*, *panch* etc. *Trya* (three) became *trias* and *panch* (five) became *pente* in Greek. The English language during the *Great Vowel Shift* used some diphthongizations like *ai* and *au*. But still the range of vowels as compared to Sanskrit was always less and incomplete and, apart from the vowels, consonants also had their own sound (like vowelless *sly, fry, dry*) which was also not always the same, like the word *chaos* where the sound of *ch* is *k* and *o* is *a*. This situation created a permanent ambiguity of the pronunciations and the vowels lost their true effects, like, *top*, *mop*, *hum, chum*, where *o* and *u* both sound as long or short *a*. Thus, a language which is developed on imperfect grounds can never be perfect, no matter how far it advances.

In Sanskrit, the basic structure of its vowel-consonant pronunciation is the unique foundation of the language that precisely stabilizes the word pronunciation where each letter (or a combination of consonants with a vowel) is a syllable.

꽃꽃꽃

2. Formation of the Sanskrit words.

The second unmatched feature is the formation of the Sanskrit words. Since the beginning we had a complete dictionary of root words called *dhatu* that could create any number of words according to the requirement by adding a proper prefix and suffix which are described in detail in the Sanskrit grammar.

The formation, modulation and creation of words have been originally the same, in an absolutely perfect state since the beginning, as they are today.

꽃꽃꽃

3. The uniqueness of the grammar.

The most impressive uniqueness of the Sanskrit grammar is that it is unchanged in every age because it is a Divinely produced grammar. Its conjugation system, word formation and the style of poetry formation are all unique, unchanged and perfectly detailed since it appeared on the earth planet through the descended Saints. Take a line of the Yajurved:

"ताँस्ते प्रेत्यभिगच्छन्ति ये के चात्महनो जनाः ॥" (ई.)

There is a noun *janah* (people), and verb *gacchanti* (to go into) which is formed of *gam dhatu* (to go), like, *gacchati, gacchatah, gacchanti*. All the 90 *conjugations* of the verb *gacch* (to go) and all the 21 forms of the noun *jan* (people) are used in the same way without any change in the Vedas, in the Puranas and in other Sanskrit literature as well, because they are ever perfect without any sound shift. The Sanskrit language represents the literal form of the Divinity on the earth planet. Such is the Sanskrit grammar.

4. The three kinds of prime Sanskrit scriptures (Vedas, Upnishads and the Puranas) and their style of literary presentation.

There are three styles of Sanskrit: (a) the Vedas (*sanhita*), (b) the Upnishads and (c) the Puranas. All of them were reproduced during the same period before 3102 BC. But their literature has its own style. The difference in the style and the uses of words in all the three kinds of scriptures does not mean any evolution or improvement in the vocabulary. It is just their style. For example, the word *khalu* has been used only once in the Rigved *sanhita.* Vedic verses do not use the full range of words as is used in the Puranas and the Bhagwatam because they are mainly the invocation *mantras* for the celestial gods and that too for ritualistic purposes, not for the devotion to supreme God. So they don't need too many words to relate a *mantra.* They have their own character, and use some of their own wordings which are unusual to regular Sanskrit literature. For example: *devebhih* in the Vedas and *devaih* (celestial gods) in common Sanskrit. Similarly, *vyoman* in the Vedas and *vyomni* (Divine dimensions) in common Sanskrit. But the formation of these words is explained in the Vedic grammar and in the Nirukt, a special book for explaining such words.

The language of the Bhagwatam is very scholarly, poetic and rich as it explains the richest philosophy of God, God's love and God realization along with its other affiliated theories. It also explains the total history of this *brahmand* and its creation. The true Divine love form of the supreme God is described in the Bhagwatam.

The language of the other 17 Puranas is less rich, and the language of the Upnishads sometimes leans towards the Vedic *sanhita* side. Now we know that the difference in the literary presentation of the Vedic *sanhita* and the Puranas are their own nature and style, they do not relate to their seniority or juniority.

꧁꧂꧁

5. The *apbhransh.*

Apbhransh (and prakrit) part of Sanskrit literature. In every society there are many classes of people. Some are educated, some are less educated and some are much less educated. Accordingly, the quality of their speech differs. Thus, during the time of Ved Vyas, when Sanskrit was the spoken language of India, there may have been some people who spoke a localized form of less perfect Sanskrit. As time went on a new language developed in the Bihar area of North India which was a combination of the localized dialect with the *apbhransh* words of Sanskrit. The pronunciation of the Sanskrit word changes when it is spoken by the people who are less educated or not educated in the Sanskrit language, and then such words permanently enter into their locally spoken language. These, partly mispronounced words, are called the *apbhransh*. Still, Sanskrit remained the spoken language of the literary class of India at least up to the time of Shankaracharya.

When Shankaracharya went to have an audience with Mandan Mishra he found two parrots in two cages that were hung in front of his house. They were happily uttering Sanskrit phrases (जगद्ध्रुवं स्याद्, जगद्ध्रुवं स्याद) which they had memorized by listening to the scriptural discussions that were usually happening in the house. All over India Shankaracharya debated in Sanskrit language wherever he went. It was around 500 BC.

That was the time when the Greek and Latin languages were in the course of their development. Trade communications between India, Persia, Mesopotamia, Syria and Greece were already well established. The stories of the Puranas and the Bhagwatam had already reached, in a broken form, into those countries which they then adopted in their society and incorporated into their religious mythology. The Iliad and the Odyssey in their earliest and incomplete forms were composed around 600 BC, and later on certain Sanskrit *apbhransh* words were added in the Greek and Latin languages (which Jones picked as examples for his speech in Calcutta).

6. Sanskrit, the scriptural language up till today.

Now we know that Sanskrit was the spoken language among the scholars up to the time of Kalidas. The disciple Saints of Chaitanya Mahaprabhu wrote hundreds of books in Sanskrit language on the supreme knowledge, beauty, love and the loving pastimes of Krishn, and Jeev Goswami described the detailed philosophy of soul, *maya* (original cosmic energy), God and the intimate eternal manifestation of God's Gracious personality of Divine love (called the *prem tattva*).

The famous debate of Lord Chaitanya with Sarvabhaum Bhattacharya that happened in the Sanskrit language established the popularity of the Sanskrit language in the educated society of India up to the 16th century AD. After 1857 when English rule tried to suppress Sanskrit education in India by introducing and encouraging English education by all means and cutting the grants for the Sanskrit colleges, Sanskrit education (being the soul of Bhartiya culture) still survived, and keeping its glory it maintained its potential. Now the Sanskrit colleges all over India are maintaining the greatness of the eternal Divine language that was introduced by the creator Brahma on this earth planet at the very beginning of human civilization.

Certain European writers and their blind followers tried to confuse the issue of the eternal perfection of the Sanskrit language.

They argued that in the beginning the language (of the Vedas) was in an undeveloped stage. Afterwards when it became a refined language then it was called the Sanskrit language. In this way they tried to prove the gradual development of the Sanskrit language. But their biased intellect failed to understand the actual significance of the word *'sanskrit.'* The word *'sanskrit'* is formed as "*sam + krit*" where *sam* prefix means (*samyak*) 'entirely' or 'wholly' or 'perfectly,' and *krit* means 'done.' **So, 'sanskrit' word means the one which is introduced or produced in its perfect form. Thus, the Sanskrit language even according to its own literal meaning proves to be a perfect language by its own character.** It was first introduced by Brahma to the Sages of the celestial abodes and still it is the language of the celestial abode, so it is also called the Dev Vani.

The latest happening of the historical representation of scholarly Sanskrit discourses was in **1957** by the Divine descension of this age, Shree Kripaluji Maharaj, that glorified God Shiv's glorious town Varanasi for seven days. It revealed the philosophies of all of our major scriptures and reconciled them with the theme of the Bhagwatam. It was such an event that enthralled the great learned *pandits* (Sanskrit scholars) of India with the sweetness of the Divine touch that was imbued in the dry looking Darshan Shastras and they wholeheartedly desired him to accept the honor of being the supreme **Jagadguru** of this age (*Jagadguruttam*) as a flower of their heartfelt appreciation.

(4) Sanskrit is the mother language of the world.

Sanskrit language, as we see is all-perfect from the very beginning when the western world didn't even have a proper alphabet.

"अन्धं तमः प्रविषन्ति येऽविद्यामुपासते ।" (ई.)

The words of the Vedas like: *vishanti, upasate* are used in the same way in the Gita and the Puranas because there has never been any change or improvement in the formation of its words as it was the self-perfected language, which is also an indication of its Divineness.

This situation itself is the authentication of this fact that Sanskrit is the first and the mother language of the world; and its unique and eternal perfection, which is unimagined and unmatched in the world, is the positive verdict of its being a Divine (supernatural) language.

It is thus established that the Sanskrit language, since its appearance in the world through Brahma, maintained the glory of our eternal scriptures in its perfect linguistic representation. All the scriptures including all the Puranas were again reproduced between 3200 and 3102 BC by Bhagwan Ved Vyas whose Divine wisdom was unlimited and whose Divine clairvoyance saw everything of past, present and future. If someone's conscience fails to comprehend the eternal authenticity of the Sanskrit language for some reason, then at least, according to the above descriptions, one can surely understand its undefied perfection that had the capacity of introducing hundreds of thousands of words according to its root system since the very beginning, when even the earliest known cursive writing systems of the world (Greek and Hebrew etc.) were at their infancy and were struggling to standardize their pronunciation and to improve their vocabulary. During that process they adopted certain *apbhransh* or commonly used words of Sanskrit which are found in almost all the languages of the world.

Then, how and why did Sir William Jones set up such a fabricated falsehood to derogate the Sanskrit language and introduce such a fictitious tale (that was later on termed as Proto-Indo-European language) in his Calcutta speech of 1786? Was he an enemy of Bhartiya culture?

No, **he was an intelligent and most obedient servant of the British regime, employed by the British diplomats to cleverly destroy the culture, religion and the history of Bharatvarsh** so that the British could rule India forever and spread their religion (Christianity), and, at the same time, they could make use of the scientific knowledge of the Vedic scriptures, whatever they could find. *Now we can learn about the social, cultural and the linguistic developments of the western world which is hardly three to five thousand years old.*

CHAPTER FOUR

History of the social and cultural developments of the western world.

(1) Early civilizations and the development of writing systems in the world.

The origin of primitive writing systems.

As a natural process of renovation of world civilizations, ice ages come. Blanketing most of the Southern and Northern Hemispheres of the earth planet with trillions of tons of ice for millions of years they bury and destroy all the civilizations in its area. It stretches up to the major parts of Europe including England. Its spine chilling below freezing winds shoot cold waves all over the continent which shatters the rest of the civilizations. **India is not much affected by the ice ages** because it is in the tropical zone and the range of the Himalayan hills protects it from the cold winds of the deep North. So its ancient civilization continues without interruption.

The last ice age receded around 10,000 years ago. It took some time to develop the normal conditions of living. The survivors of the ice age were small groups of people who were living a nomadic life. They spread all over the southern parts of Europe and the middle parts of Asia, the Gulf countries, some parts of North America, South America and Africa.

Sumerians and the first writing system in the world.

The earliest known records show the presence of some village people in the north of Mesopotamia around 7000 BC. People were also living in the Sumer region of south Mesopotamia since 5000 BC. Later on some more people came and settled in Sumer. The Sumerians developed a form of *pictographic* writing that used word pictures like bird, fish, ox or grain etc., around 4000 - 3500 BC. In 3000 BC, it developed into a cursive form of *cuneiform* style of writing which was a wedge shaped linear impression on clay tablets.

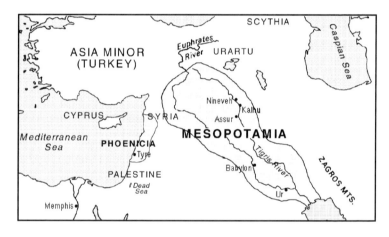

Cuneiform writing was first in pictographic type. After the 3rd millennium BC it took a conventional form of linear cuneiform drawings and was written from left to right. Akkadian, Aramaic, Persian and also other languages of the Middle East were written in cuneiform. Since the time of Christ the knowledge about the Sumerians and their language was totally forgotten and vanished from the history. It was known only after 1800 AD when the cuneiform script was deciphered. The first one was Semitic-Babylonian Akkadian language and the other was the Persian language. It was then that the correct name 'Sumerian' was given to the Sumerian language. *The cuneiform writing dates between the 3rd millennium and 2nd century BC. It could be categorized as: (1) Sumerian cuneiform, (2) Babylonian cuneiform and (3) Assyrian cuneiform.*

Egyptian language, religion and gods.

Egyptians borrowed the idea of pictorial writing from Sumerians. Their writing, which was introduced in 3000 BC, was called hieroglyphics and was styled as pictography or ideograms. It had about 700 signs and was written mainly from right to left but occasionally from left to right or top to downward. Original hieroglyphics were developed into phonetic hieroglyphs like the characters of an alphabet. But it had no vowels so, even after deciphering the words, it was not possible to know their actual pronunciations. Around 1100 BC it was changed to a newly developed cursive style called the *'hieratic,'* and then in about 700 BC it was changed to *'demotic.'*

'Demotic' language was replaced by Coptic around 200 AD which was written in Greek alphabet with seven letters borrowed from 'demotic.' It had six dialects, four of the north and two of the south of Egypt. Finally, around 640 AD, after the Arab invasion, Arabic language and the Arabic script was introduced in Egypt and the Coptic language was replaced by 1200 AD.

Egyptian language is an extinct language that belonged to the Hamito-Semitic language family. For a very long time these writings remained unintelligible until a big stone slab with three detailed inscriptions in three scripts (hieroglyphic, demotic and Greek) was found in 1799 AD near Rosetta town near the mouth of the River Nile.

Thanks to the Rosetta stone that it revealed the Egyptian culture and the history, otherwise they would have been buried under the blanket of linguistic ignorance. Egypt had a number of gods and goddesses. The main ones were: *Re* (a male figure with a cat/bird/lion's head), the chief sun god; *Ptah* (a mummified man with a shaven head); *Bast* (a cat-headed woman); *Isis* (a female form with horn and a vulture headdress), the queen of gods; *Mut* (a female figure with a vulture head or headdress), their divine mother.

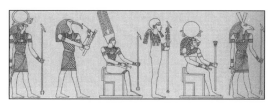

Sumerians and Babylonians.

As the Sumerian language developed and more words were added, the representation of words became more and more complicated, still it had only 16 consonants and four vowels (a, e, i and u). In general, the Sumerian civilization flourished between 3500 to 2200 BC. They made palaces and temples and established cities (the main city was Ur). Around 2200 BC the Babylonian Semites invaded Sumer and ruled up to 539 BC. Then Persians conquered the region and ruled until Alexander invaded Babylonia in 331 BC and enormously expanded his kingdom from Greece to the west of India. Alexander made **Babylon** the capital of his realm and died there in 323 BC. After Alexander's death Babylonia crumbled. Babylonia was one of the kingdoms of Mesopotamia situated in the south of it and its main town was Babylon.

(An example of Sumerian writing systems)					(An example of Egyptian writing systems)			
original pictograph	later pictograph	early Babylonian cuneiform	Assyrian cuneiform	derived meaning	Hiero-glyphic	Approximate name	Hieratic	Demotic
🐦				bird		eagle		
				fish		leaf		
				ox		owl		
				grain		water		
				to stand to go		stand		

The **Babylonian kingdom** was established around 2200 BC and ended by 323 BC. It had seen two major attacks; one by the Assyrians in 700 BC when Babylonia saw its worst days and remained disturbed up to 612 BC, and the other by the Persians in 539 BC who took the power and ruled up to 331 BC.

The Babylonian kingdom expanded its empire mainly after 1750 BC, built a huge castle, developed commercial activities and traded its goods. A major change came after 612 BC when the new Babylonian Empire gradually gained control over most of the neighboring areas and achieved its greatest glory. It had a fort-like palace with eight bronze gates, and there were roads, buildings, paved avenues and the temple of *their chief god Marduk who was the thunder and rain deity and the lord of heaven and earth.* There were more than 250,000 people living in Babylon and nearby places. It was the wealthiest and the largest commercial center in the Middle East at that time. *In those days there were hundreds of gods that were worshipped in the society. Some were Semitic gods, some were Sumerian gods and some were Babylonian gods.*

Sumerian periods could be classified as: Archaic (up to 2500 BC), Old or Classical (up to 2300 BC), New (up to 2000 BC), and Post-Sumerian (after 2000 BC). The Sumerian language flourished up to 2200 BC. But, when the Babylonian Semites came to power, a Northeastern Semitic language, called Akkadian, became the common language of Assyria and Babylonia. It was thus called Assyro-Babylonian Akkadian language. Although it was introduced as a spoken language, the cuneiform system of writing was still being used. Lots of cuneiform clay tablets have been found in Semite and Persian language that show that it was the common system of writing of ancient Middle East civilization, but slowly, as other languages came into being and after the downfall of Babylonia after 323 BC, the Sumerian language and the cuneiform script died out.

The Assyrians.

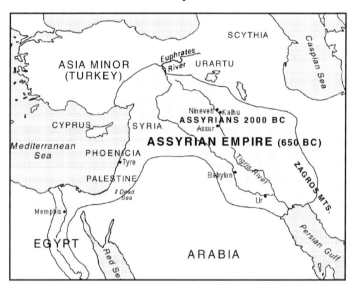

Northern Mesopotamia (North Iraq) was called Assyria. The ancient Assyrian people were of an unknown race, living in small villages around 5000 to 4000 BC. Its civilization was somewhat similar to ancient Babylonia but it had a better climate for agriculture. Before 3000 BC the Semite group of people came and settled over there. They were a mixture of many races, and spoke Semitic language (that is related to Hebrew or Arabic of today). The Assyrian kingdom was like a dependency of Babylonia for most of the time up to 2nd millennium BC, but very little is known about early Assyrian people. It became an independent kingdom around 1400 BC, briefly expanded its kingdom between 1200 to 1000 BC, but after 800 BC it expanded considerably, and, between 744 and 670 BC, it conquered all the states from Babylonia to Egypt. After 635 BC a civil war broke out and then Babylonians attacked in 614 BC which finally ended the Assyrian empire.

Assyrians built palaces, cities and temples with beautiful carved stone slabs that showed religious ceremonies. Assur was the main town named after their chief god **Assur** or Ashur. *They also believed in many gods, like the god of learning, god of war, goddess of love etc., and their religion was similar to Babylonian religion.* They also worshipped many gods. Assyrians, Babylonians and Sumerians, they all believed in a number of gods and in this way there were hundreds of gods being worshipped in the community. They also believed that the king is the representative of god on earth, but the Assyrian king was known as the king of kings whose territory was all the four corners of the earth, from the upper sea to the lower sea.

Early Assyrians spoke Akkadian language which was Northern peripheral or Northeastern Semitic language spoken between 3rd to 1st millennium BC in Mesopotamia. It had two dialects, Assyrian and Babylonian. That's why it was called 'Assyro-Babylonian' language. It was written in cuneiform script. After 700 BC the Aramaic language, which was a Northern central Semitic language, began to replace the Akkadian language, and thus, it completely died out by 1st century AD. Its cuneiform script was deciphered only after 1799 AD. The Aramaic of the late Assyrians was written in both scripts, the Aramaic script as well as the cuneiform script. Thus both scripts survived.

The Semites.

People who originally lived on the eastern side of the Mediterranean spoke a kind of language that was called Semite, thus, the Semite-speaking people were called the Semites. Hebrew and Arabic are the main descendents of the Semitic language. The Semite people lived mainly in what is now called Israel, Jordan, Syria, Lebanon (Phoenicia) and Iraq (Mesopotamia), then they moved to Arabia and North Africa. Ancient Assyrians, Babylonians, Hebrews and the Canaanites of Canaan were also Semites. Canaan was the Biblical name for the land on the East Mediterranean coastal area around the Dead Sea and the Jordan river. It was also called Palestine. Judaism and Christianity originated from there.

Before 3000 BC those people were living in the Northern part, afterwards they moved to the South. Northwestern Semites spoke mainly Hebrew and Aramaic language. (The ancient Israelites, who lived in Palestine in Biblical times and who spoke Hebrew and wrote in Hebrew, were called the Hebrews.) Southern Semites spoke Arabic. There were many dialects and a number of offshoots of Aramaic and Arabic languages.

(2) The origin of alphabets and the languages of the world.

The origin of alphabets.

Linguists have no idea how, when and where the languages of the world began, diverged, or mixed; because they did not look towards the Sanskrit language whose vowel system was partly adopted by the Greeks and whose *apbhransh* words are still found in the languages of the world. They believe that Semites and Greeks are the main people who originated and developed the alphabetic system of writing which is used by most of the languages of the world. *Semitic system had only consonants, Greeks added vowels to it.* The North Semitic Phoenicians developed the first form of graphic signs around 1500 BC and the Greeks developed the vowel system of alphabetic writing around 800 BC (see diagram pp. 96 & 126).

Phoenician and Greek alphabets and languages.

The earliest (deciphered) **Phoenician** inscription is of 1100 BC. Phoenicia is the coastal part of Canaan (now called Lebanon) and it had the earliest and easiest readable inscriptions. That's how it became the ancestor of all the western alphabets. **Phoenicians and Hebrews were the tribes of Canaan** that settled there from about 3000 BC. Thus, the style of their alphabet was also called the Canaanite.

The **Phoenician** language is now extinct. It was spoken on the mainland from 2000 to 1000 BC. It barely survived in certain Mediterranean islands until early Christian centuries, and then became extinct. They spoke a dialect of **Northern Central Semite** language that was related to Hebrew and used the cuneiform script of writing. **Later they developed their own alphabet that had 22 consonants but no vowels** in about 1600 BC. They were seagoing traders, good ship builders and sailors, believed in many gods and practiced sacrifices as other Semitic people did. They gathered many mythological tales of creation and flood etc. from the Babylonians. They specialized in ivory and wood carving and metal works, and their trading expeditions reached up to Spain where they established colonies along their southern coast. The Phoenician language was superceded by the Aramaic language during the 1st century BC.

The Greeks. Around 900 BC the Greeks adopted Semitic (Phoenician) graphic-signs which were a kind of mixed consonant-vowel syllabic single-character type. Their graphic-signs were based on the idea of representing a *single specific sound used to indicate the commonly known objects and things; and they were kept in a series of 22 signs. They were like an individual speech sound instead of syllables. For example, their sound for ox was 'aleph* which was a single sound but that 'one single sound' collectively incorporated the sound images of all the letters of *'aleph*. That may have been enough for the people of those days when they needed to speak or write in a very limited scope. Although it was an inefficient system of writing, still it was a great creation of the Phoenicians which became the guideline for introducing a true alphabetic writing.

The Greeks took the 22 names and their graphic-signs with some modifications. For example: the Phoenician letter pronounced as *'aleph* (meant for *ox*) became *alpha* of Greek; and *beth* (meant for *house*) became *beta* of Greek.

Later on they refined and enhanced their alphabetic system. They deleted four letters (signs) out of the twenty-two which had some kind of ambiguity. Again, they used six of their letters (signs) to represent the correct sound of the vowels and added six new letters to their alphabet, thus making it a twenty-four letter alphabet.

Descendants of Greek alphabet.

The **direct descendants** of Greek alphabet are Etruscan, Latin (and Romance) and Cyrillic. The language used by the **Etruscan** people was called the Etruscan language. They were the inhabitants of western Italy (now Tuscany) sometime before 900 BC. Their language is now extinct and not yet understood. In the beginning they used Greek (Phoenician) alphabet of 22 signs (with Greek phonetic values) and later on added 4 more letters, thus making it 26. Etruscan writing was always from right to left. The earliest inscription of their writing is of 8th century BC. The Etruscan alphabet had several offshoots and it did not have a fixed standard of writing. It went through many changes. However, after 400 BC the classical Etruscan alphabet took its final shape of 20 letters, 16 consonants and 4 vowels. The language is still undeciphered. They were very prosperous between 500-400 BC, traded their handcrafted goods in the Mediterranean area and believed in sacrifices. The communities living in Latium (near Rome) came into their contact around 700 BC. Etruscan kings ruled early Rome, but after 300 BC the Roman conquest totally finished their kingships.

Latin alphabet was taken from Greek through Etruscan affiliation around 700-600 BC. They took 21 letters from the Etruscan (Greek) alphabet including *k*. Later on *y* and *z* were added to it around 1st century BC when the Romans took over Greece. Thus, the Classic Latin had a 23 letter alphabet. In the medieval times during the development of Old English, the letter *i* was exaggerated as *i* and *j*, and *v* as *u*, *v* and *w*; thus making it a 26 letter alphabet.

Early writings of Latin ran from right to left. Later on they developed their writing system and borrowed a great number of Greek words. *The languages that were developed from Latin are called the Romance languages.*

Based on the Greek alphabet the Cyrillic alphabet was created by two Greek brothers for Slavic speaking people like Russians,

Ukrainians, Bulgarians and Serbs, etc. Originally it had 42 letters but it was reduced according to the needs of the language of that country, for instance, Russian has 32 and Bulgarian has only 30 letters. There are more than twenty Slavic languages (with their dialects) and each one has its own grammar and vocabulary.

Hebrew, Aramaic, Arabic and Persian alphabets and languages.

Hebrew language is one of the oldest known languages of the world. Early Hebrew language was closely related to Phoenician language which had a 22 letter alphabet and no vowels. It was spoken by the Hebrews of Palestine since the 13th century BC. Later on, between 600 and 300 BC, the Hebrew language was under the influence of Aramaic language, so the style of Hebrew writing was changed to Aramaic script. Some parts of the Old Testament were written in early Hebrew, but the sections of the Old Testament written in that period were in Aramaic script.

The collection of the description of Jewish traditional rules about religious prayers, marriage and rules of family living, civil laws, temple sacrifices and offerings etc. is called *Mishna*, which is supposed to have been orally produced between 600-400 BC. *Talmud* (100-500 AD) is the explanation of the religious beliefs, and *Torah* generally refers to the first five books of Moses.

The period of **Early Hebrew** could be given to be around 1000 BC and of **Aramaic Hebrew** up to around 300 BC. After 300 BC there was a major development in the writing structures of Hebrew language and a new style of alphabet, like a cross between the alphabets of early Hebrew and Aramaic Hebrew was developed which displaced the Aramaic alphabet probably before 200 BC. It was called **Square Hebrew.**

During the Christian era the language was further modified and standardized, and, around 7th century AD, proper vowels (as dot and dash) were added to it. It took more than 1,500 years to take the shape of Modern Hebrew alphabet and the language as well. Square Hebrew scripts are found mostly between 800 and 1400 AD. **Modern Hebrew** is a refined version of Square Hebrew. It has a 26 letter alphabet out of which some are stressed ones like *kaph, khaph* and *seen* and *sheen*. Apart from *aleph, he, waw* and *yod*, which were employed as long vowels in Square Hebrew, there are quite a few vowel signs that are also used in Modern Hebrew writing. They are dot and dash under or on the top of a letter like:

It is written from right to left. As a spoken language Hebrew declined from the 9th century until the 18th century. It revived again in the 19th and 20th centuries, and now it is the official language of Israel.

Aramaic: The oldest **Aramaic** inscriptions belong to the 9th century BC. Aramaic was the spoken language of the North Semitic people living in northern Mesopotamia and Syria since the 13th century BC. The script that developed around 1000 BC to write the Aramaic language was called the Aramaic alphabet. It writes right to left and has 22 letters, all consonants. Square Hebrew, Arabic and Persian alphabets were developed from Aramaic. Some of the Dead Sea Scrolls are in Aramaic script (150 BC).

Jesus and his apostles spoke the Aramaic language.

A sample of latest Aramaic script: ‏ﻻﺅﻣﺮﺍ ﻣﺄﻓﺘﻌﺘﺎ ﻻ ﻧﺪﺟﻨﺰﻭﻥ ﺣﻢ ﺣﻨﻊ‎

Arabic script was evolved around 4th century AD by the Aramaic speaking people of northern Arabia. The Arabic language (related to the Southern Central Semitic group, mainly spoken in Arabia) originated before the 5th century BC.

The colloquial Arabic has a number of spoken dialects of which some of them are mutually unintelligible and are spread around Middle East, Arabia, Iraq, Syria, Egypt, Algeria and North Africa etc.

Persian: The Persian language belongs to the **Iranian** group of languages. The earliest civilization of **Persia** goes back to around 3000 BC. Later on some tribes of nomads came from around the southern Soviet Union and settled in Persia (now Iran) in about 1000 BC and slowly created an empire which saw its peak in 600 BC, extending its territory from North Africa (Egypt) to the western parts of India. But, it lost its glory when Arabs conquered it in 641 AD. Its linguistic development could be divided into three periods: *(1) Old Persian (up to 300 BC) which used cuneiform script; (2) Middle Persian, also called the Pahlavi, (3rd century BC to 9th century AD) which used Aramaic alphabet for writing; and (3) Modern Persian which used Arabic alphabet.* The Persian language went through many changes in its alphabet, style of writing, vocabulary and also the grammar. The Modern Persian grammar is much simpler as compared to Pahlavi or Old Persian which has no comparison with the present system of writing. Persians follow Zoroastrianism named after Prophet Zoroaster who emphasized on one god Ahura Mazdah which means "the wise spirit." His teachings, called '*gatha*,' are collected in *Avesta* that tells about the religious rituals, prayers, sacrifices, ritual rules, civil laws of good and evil, and fire ceremonies etc. Their followers are called 'Parsis' in India. They worship fire as a representation of Ahura Mazdah.

Avesta and Pahlavi.

The period of Prophet Zoroaster is very much disputed as being sometime between 1400 BC and 600 BC. But the majority of opinion is that he was born in the early 600's and according to their religious belief he was assassinated at the age of 77. He is believed to have written his teachings called Avesta, which of course must be in cuneiform script, and as such, it must have been in small pieces of writings. Later on the Zoroastrians kept on adding their writings to it. Zoroastrianism declined after 300 BC and was further suppressed after 600 AD due to Muslim conquest.

Due to political disturbances the greater part of the original **Avesta** was lost. From the remaining fragments and from the royal favor between 531 and 578 AD it was reconstructed, expanded and redesigned in the form of a proper book in the **Middle Persian (Pahlavi) language** in Aramaic script. But most of its parts were again destroyed by the Muslim conquest in 641 AD when they changed the entire culture of the state, the script, the religion, and everything.

Pahlavi language in which Avesta is written has a lot of Sanskrit words and its *apbhransh* as well, and also the description of the deities and the style of the rituals in Avesta sometimes resemble the Vedic rituals to some extent. The reason is that its homeland Iran is very close to India (called Aryavart) where Sanskrit was the main scholarly language. At one time in the remote past the whole area from Iran to Indonesia was the land of *Aryavart.* In Indonesia the stage shows of Bhagwan Ram's story from the Ramayan are still being played in their own style every day as their national historic culture. The word *'gatha'* used in Avesta itself is the *apbhransh* of the Sanskrit word *granth*, which was commonly used by the Buddhist writers.

Early Alphabets Phoenician to early Latin					Latest Latin or modern Roman alphabet
Phoenician		Early Hebrew	Early Greek	Early Latin	
𝑋	aleph (ox)	ᚠ	ᐱ	ᐱ	A
𝟡	beth (house)	𝟫	ᗷ	B	B
ᔿ	gimel (camel)	ᐸ	𝟣	𝐶	C
ᕀ	daleth (door)	ᕾ	Δ	D	D
ᔓ	he	ᕘ	ᕃ	ᕪ	E
Ꮞ	waw (hook)*	𝅘	–	ᕫ	F
𝐼	gimel (camel)	=	I	C	G
Ⱨ	heth	ᗝ	日	H	H
⊗	–	Ꮯ	⊗	–	
𐤆	yodh (hand)	𝅘	ᒽ	I	I,J
𑁦	kaph (hollow of hand)	𝅘	ᒽ	K	K
𝑙	lamedh	𝑙	𝟣	V	L
ᒼ	mem (water)	𝅘	ᒼ	M	M
𝅘	nun (fish)	𝅘	𝅘	N	N
O	ayin (eye)	𝒪	O	O	O
𝟩	pe (mouth)	ᒥ	ᒥ	Γ	P
ᒽ	–	ᒼ	M	–	
𐤒	qoph (monkey)	ᗱ	φ	Q	Q
ᔑ	resh (head)	ᕊ	𝟣	ᖁ	R
W	shin (tooth)	ᗯ	ᒥ	ᖕ	S
ᵗ✗	taw (mark)	✗	ᐱ	T	T
(Ꮞ)	waw	–	ᒼ	V	U,V,W
ᚨ	samekh (fish)	𝅘	Ɨ	✗	X Y,Z

* Sign Ꮞ (waw) represented *F* and was the ancestor of *U,V,W* and also *Y*.

106

(3) Greek civilization, language, and literature.

After adopting Phoenician graphic-alphabet in 900 BC the Greeks employed a vowel system and added six more letters to make it a 24 letter alphabet. Earlier, what was pronounced as 'b,' now in Modern Greek it is pronounced as 'v.' It took a long time to develop the letters. There were many Greek dialects and there were certain differences in their style of writing. Lastly the Ionian style of lettering was adopted in general and **after 400 BC the letters became uniform.** The literature and art flourished mainly in the Classical Greek period.

Phonology. Although the dialects of Greek were mutually intelligible within a normal limit of understanding but the pronunciations of words and accents differed from period to period and from dialect to dialect. The short and long sounds of vowels also varied in different dialects and the political situations in the country also brought many changes with the intermigration of the dialects. But, **during the establishment of Alexander's empire in the 4th century BC and after the breakdown of old political barriers, a uniformity took place in the spoken language. This form of language was called the Koine** (means the common language) or Hellenistic Greek (400 BC - 600 AD). It replaced the other dialects and the speaking and writing systems were much standardized.

Grammar also changed in different periods. A change of language is noticed in the writings of Plato and Demosthenes. The spoken language still kept on changing even during the period of Byzantine empire (500-1500 AD) and the written language kept on improving which created a big rift between the local vernacular and the literary Greek. This situation gave birth to a separate kind of 'Demotic' language of general everyday use.

All the major phonological and grammatical changes which are seen between **Koine** and the **Modern Greek** mostly happened within this period. **Earlier there were three numbers for pronouns and verbs, singular, dual and plural. Then 'dual' was dropped and, only singular and plural were left.**

From Ancient Greek to Modern Greek the formation of many words were also changed. For example: The ancient Greek word *pente* (five) became *pende, hepta* and *okto* (seven and eight) became *efta* and *okhto, paidia* (boys) became *pedhya* and so on. There were also semantic changes in certain words, just as: the word *alogho* which previously meant '*irrational*,' later it meant 'horse;' *skiazome* which previously meant '*I am in shadow*,' later it meant 'I fear.'

The **vocabulary** of Greek language consists of local collections and borrowings. Considering the origin of Greek, there were many Mycenaean words in 2nd millennium BC whose original form corresponded to certain Greek words like *leon* (lion), *onos* (ass), *elephas* (ivory) etc.

By using preverbs, by forming compounds and by adding prefixes or suffixes to these prime words they enriched their vocabulary. Later on they also borrowed a considerable number of words from other sources, such as, Italian, Turkish, French and also Latin.

※※※

Culture and literature of Greece.

Greece was the origin of western civilization that started about 3,000 years ago. The peak of its glory was around 500 BC which was the golden age for Athens. Democritus, Socrates and his disciple Plato were in the *5th century BC* and Aristotle was in the *4th century BC*. **Democritus** introduced the theory of the creation of the universe with the atoms; **Socrates** told about the general universal principles and about one Divinity (but he was sentenced to death by drinking poison for telling the truth which they called unorthodox); **Plato** believed in the immortality of the soul and introduced his reasonings based on his idea of the intellect part of the being and the desire part of the being. He started a school of philosophy in Athens called "Academy." His pupil **Aristotle** explained in his theory of physics about the constant change in every form, phase and aspect of creation which is the inherent nature of this world, but only God is unchanged and eternal. He used the word *theology* for the philosophy of God.

The two fiction stories the Iliad and the Odyssey written in a long poetry form are famous which are traditionally believed to be composed by a blind but imaginative bard, Homer (alone or together with his traveling friend), around 700 BC and were recited in the community. Between 300 and 100 BC from the available handwritten parts of the Iliad and the Odyssey and from the prevailing recited stories, the existing books that are available nowadays, were compiled, edited and again properly written.

༔༔༔

The Iliad and the Odyssey of Homer.

The **Iliad** is a fancied description of the last part of the legendary Trojan war (in twenty-four small sections) that went on for 10 years (around 1350 BC) between the Greek army and the king of Troy to rescue Helen (the Queen of Sparta) who was abducted by the son of the king of Troy. The characters of the story are fictitious and the plot of the story follows the imagination of the writer. The story ends with Hector's funeral who was leading the Greek forces in the end.

The **Odyssey** is also in the ancient style of Greek poetry. This imaginative story describes the adventures of King Odysseus (the main character of the fiction story) in a heroic way when he is returning back to his home after fighting a battle. The story also portrays the lust, jealousy and the revengefulness of the gods who were produced by the imagination of Homer and which became the guidelines for portraying the gods of the Greek mythology.

The story starts from the middle, where, after seven years of captivation by a sea nymph, the hero of the play, Odysseus, gains the favor of the chief god Zeus and goddess Athena and, with the help of Hermes, he comes out of the captivity and sails forward in a raft. But, the god of the sea, Poseidon, ragefully capsizes the raft by causing a sea storm because he had killed one of his demon friends on one of the islands where he stayed during his journey. He was washed ashore by the waves when a princess finds him and takes him to her homeland.

Prior to those happenings he went through a number of adventures that happened in various imaginary lands that were inhabited with people having magic powers and also there were some demons on certain islands. Once when he landed on an island the lady enchantress of that island made his people pigs and Odysseus her lover. With her help he visits the underworld where he sees ghosts of his mother and the people who died in war. Later on as he proceeds with his men towards his country, the god's rage in the form of a violent thunderbolt destroys the ship along with his people because some of his men had stealthily eaten the cattle of the sun god on one of the islands. He is washed ashore on the island of Ogygia, the land of the sea nymph, from where the story started. Finally he comes home after ten years of tragic life and joins his wife.

Such stories give an idea of the society and the people of those days and also their beliefs. It is a fact that the ancient Greeks laid the foundation of western civilization. They also contributed to the knowledge of biology, geometry, history, philosophy, physics and the logics of Plato, fine arts, architecture and music. The temple of Athena (450 BC) is famous for its architecture.

The golden age of Athens began to decline when the Peloponnesian war broke out in 431 BC and shortly after that the epidemic of plague killed one third of the Athenians, but, during the reign of Alexander it again regained its prosperity. However, the expanding powerful conquests of the Roman Empire took over Macedonia (Greece) in 148 BC and there were lots of disturbances and destructions in Greece during that time.

༺༺༺

The origin of Homer's mythological imaginations and the religion of Greece.

In ancient times there were trade connections between the eastern Mediterranean countries, Persia and India, and also people traveled long distances in those days. Thus, the social culture of India and certain popular stories of the Puranas, like: **(ब्रह्मा द्वारा सृष्टि, मनु शतरूपा, देवासुर संग्राम, प्रलय दर्शन, आकाश वाणी, इन्द्रदि देवताओं के व्यवहार)** the creation of celestial and material world by Brahma, first material sky then the earth; the first originators of human civilization Manu and Shatroopa; wars between gods and demons in the celestial plane; the story of water deluge that flooded the whole world (dissolving the celestial abodes also) when Rishi Satyavrat kept the subtle bodies of all the souls with him and stayed in the ship during the previous *kalp pralaya*; the story of gods and goddesses when they went to Vishnu's abode and there they heard a Divine voice; and the stories of god Indra, Varun, Kamdeo, Kuber, Agni, Vayu and the creator Brahma etc. traveled through sea routes. Also, many other commonly known stories of the Indian community reached these countries by word of mouth with some additions and subtractions as they traveled from mouth to mouth and the people of these countries incorporated them in their mythologies.

For example: the story of water deluge (*pralaya*) became 'the great flood' of the Bible, and the stories and the epithets of our celestial gods and goddesses became the source of their imagination about mythologizing the characters of gods and

goddesses in their religion and worship. Thus, we find that Assyrians, Babylonians, Sumerians, Semites, Egyptians and Greeks, all of them believed and worshipped many gods and goddesses with somewhat similar characters like god of rain and storm (Zeus), god of love (Eros), god of underworld (Hades), goddess of fire (Hestia), and goddess of wisdom (Athena), etc. Zeus was their chief god. In addition to that they also created many more gods and goddesses with their own imaginations. The forms and features of their gods and goddesses were created either in a human form or a combination of human and animal form (as Egyptian gods), whatever befitted according to their nature, imagination and social living.

We find that the ancient society of Greece had adopted certain social customs that were prevailing in India. Such as: the husband headed the family and the wife ran the household affairs; parents arranged and decided their children's marriage; a girl was controlled and protected by her parents before marriage and by her husband after marriage; and many more such customs.

(4) The history of the origination of the concepts of the words 'god/God' in the west.

god/God.

There are varying and unsure theories how the word for 'god' was primarily coined in various languages and cultures. But all of them come to one general assumption that they all indicated towards the presence of some kind of nature-spirit or some superior being which was assumed to have superhuman powers.

In Greek language the word for god was presumably created from some adjective that was implicated to mean 'sacred, separate from daily routine,' and in Latin, a noun referring to the idea of a 'luminous sky' was used to form the word for god. In Germanic, the word for god was constructed from a root-verb meaning 'to invoke' or 'to call.'

The **Old Testament** was written in the **Hebrew** language, but the **New Testament** (including the gospels) was written in **Greek**. In the early 400's, it was translated into **Latin**, and in the middle ages it was again translated into English (a Germanic language), and also into other languages.

In **Hebrew** language, *el, elohim* and *eloah,* all the three words mean god (or God) according to the person's own concept. Originally *elohim* meant gods as a collective noun, but from the time of Biblical Hebrew it began to be used for one single God. There was no system of using capital letters in the early days, and even today the Hebrew Bible uses small '*e*' for *el* or *elohim* or *eloah*. There is no word with female gender for god in Hebrew.

In **Greek** language there is a word *'theos'* that is used for *god* or *gods*, and also for *God*. It literally means 'the sacred' or 'the object of prayer.' Primarily it was meant for Zeus or any other Greek god. In Classical Greek it was used for god/gods. In Classical Greek there is no capitalization of words. In Modern Greek only in the beginning of a paragraph or in the names of certain important personalities or in the headline of a chapter, the first letter is capitalized. The word theos is not capitalized even in the latest Bible. It just means god or gods or God, and it is masculine gender; *thea* means goddess and *theai* means goddesses.

In **Latin** language the word *'deus'* is meant for god or deity which is derived from the word *'deiuos'* which refers to the idea of a luminous sky (a shiny thing or some kind of heaven). The Latin language took its literary shape between 200-100 BC.

In common **Germanic,** also called Teutonic language, (before 800 AD) there was a word *'gutha'* that was used for 'god.' It meant the invoked being, *guth* (single) and *gutha* (plural). Pagans also used the word *guth/gutha* for god/gods. It was formed from the root verb *ghu* (to invoke), and *ghu* was a variation of its ancestor *hu* (to call, to invoke). *Gutha* word was later called *gud* in Swedish, Danish and old Norse; and in Old High German and Middle High German it was written as *gut*. In the modern High **German** it was written as *Gott*. The same is in modern German; and in English it is 'God' which is singular masculine. In the beginning *'Gott'* was neutral gender (it), then it began to be used as a singular masculine noun. Plural for *Gott* is *Götter*, and its feminine word is *Göttin/ Göttinen* for goddess/goddesses. The word *Gott* means: (1) The Greek or Roman god. (2) The highest being with superhuman and supernatural powers and the object of religious faith and worship.

According to the above descriptions it is evident that the general concept of the word 'god' originated from the idea of propitiating an unknown 'spirit' of nature by prayingly calling it and invoking it in order to gain its favor for the fulfillment of some of one's own personal desires. Those nature spirits or nature energies were referred to with different words in different languages. The concept of the individualized nature spirits was the creation of the imaginations of Homer who gave them proper names (like Zeus etc.) and imagined them in human forms with supernatural powers and with humanlike emotions of love, hate and anger. They were called god and goddess whose wrath was supposed to be disastrous for mankind.

This ideology gave rise to many kinds and classes of *mythological gods and goddesses which were being worshipped and invoked with elaborate animal sacrifices in various countries in those days.* Although Moses gave a new concept of only one God instead of many gods to his people, but the basic form of elaborate animal sacrifices at the altar remained the same. Jesus gave his preachings against the animal sacrifices at the altar. Still, the wrathful nature of the kind God has been described in the Revelation, Matthew and John etc. Thus, *from Homer to the writers of the New Testament the metaphysical nature of god/ God as being the 'spirit' (of either an individual aspect of nature like 'god of rain,' or god of the whole world) remained the same.* Only certain attributes and the style of writing the word '*god/God*' changed.

In Aramaic and Greek the term god is written with small 'g.' Latin and English translations of the Bible started to write it with capital 'G.' The Old Testament in English wrote only 'God,' and the New Testament in English began to write Father God. Homer mentioned gods as individual 'spirits' of the nature, but the 'spirit God' of the whole world (in Old and New Testament) was attributed with the creatorship of this world. That was all that differed. **Still, the word God remained as an undefined 'spirit.'**

Thus, up to the period of the New Testament the concept and the definition of God remained only on the metaphysical level with the ambiguity of imagination that 'it' may be 'he' of some unknown form, yet 'its' definition remained only as a *'spirit,'* having a wrathful and vengeful nature with the power of judgement where the true laws of the wrongs and the rights are not systematically defined.

That spirit-like metaphysical cosmic power (the 'spirit' God) was supposed to be the creator of the world and its dwelling place was called the 'heaven.' Homer imagined his imaginative gods to be living in the space of an assumed dimension called the Olympus mountain. The terms 'Father' and 'the kingdom of God' of the New Testament were not properly defined, so they had no definite tangible meaning.

Theologians of the world introduced their speculated theories from time to time, and, in the middle ages, the definition of God broadened a little, but still it remained in the realm of the universal metaphysical (cosmic) energy. Even today the modern English dictionary defines God as *the supreme being and the ultimate reality, creator and ruler of the universe, eternal, omnipotent and infinite.*

The true definition of God.

There are two eternal powers involved in the creation of the universe: (1) The absolute supreme Gracious God and (2) the metaphysical universal energy, the cosmic power, called *maya.* *Maya*, being initially lifeless, receives its enlivenment from the supreme Gracious God and then manifests the entire universe.

The true and absolute supreme God has four most important personal virtues. He is ***all-Gracious, all-kind, all-Blissful and all-loving***, and, with all of His virtues, He is ***omnipresent***. Apart from that He is also *almighty* because the mighty power *maya* is under Him. He is the *creator* because He enlivens the power, *maya*, which manifests the universe, He is *omniscient* because He knows each and every action of the unlimited lives of all the unlimited souls of this universe; and so on.

One other question that has puzzled the theologians for millenniums is: whether God is He, or She, or it?

Bhartiya scriptures say that He is all. He is He as well as She, and Both forms, She and He, are absolutely one and synonymous. That's how, being absolutely one, They always remain in two forms, She and He.

What about 'it'? How does 'He' become 'it'? The answer is, that He doesn't become 'it.' *'It,' in fact, is an aspect of the personal form of God.* 'It' is such an aspect where all of His powers and attributes are absolutely dormant. It's like a person who is deeply sleeping in a dreamless state where all the dignity of his being, including his personal identity, is fully submerged into his totally inactive state. This aspect of God is called *nirgun nirakar*, which means virtueless and formless God; the other one is called *sagun sakar* (or *sakar*), which means the all-virtuous personified form of God. Thus, *sakar* **is the main form of God**, and, with His *sakar* form, He/ She is omnipresent with all of the virtues: Graciousness, kindness, all-Blissfulness, all-lovingness and many more. These Divine situations and existences are the Divine miracles that are beyond the material logic because they are beyond the realm of 'time' and 'space' factors.

Now we know that unless the **above mentioned attributes and virtues along with the prominence of the personal form of God** are included in the general meaning of the word 'God,' it would not represent the true Gracious God, it would only represent the absolute metaphysical energy of the cosmos *(and up till now these facts have not yet been incorporated into any of the English dictionaries).*

⁂⁂⁂

CHAPTER FIVE

Origin and the characteristics of the myths of the world.

(1) What is a myth?

We should now understand what a myth is. **Myth is the imaginative fiction of the minds of the ancient natives of a country who believed that there were some kind of nature gods who were involved in the creation, maintenance and destruction of the world, and in some way they also influenced the social life of the people.** Thus, they formulated imaginative stories about them and started worshipping them in their own style by offering sacrifices of such animals which they themselves used to eat.

There are thousands of mythologies. Every country in the world has a number of mythologies. Their imaginations about the shape of god also differ from country to country. For example, Greek gods are portrayed in human form, whereas the Egyptian gods are portrayed as having a human body with a human or an animal head and with a peculiar dress. There are all kinds of mythologies: cosmogony or creation myth, myth about the last judgement and death, myth of the destruction of the world, myth of human generation like of Adam and Eve, myth about the period of creation, just like the Zoroastrians of ancient Persia believed in four periods of 3,000 years (12,000 years) only, myth about the soul leaving the body after death, just like the Egyptians believed that the soul flies out from the body like a bird after death, and many more.

(2) Characteristics of the myths of the world.

There are eight main characteristics of the myths. (1) They have no philosophy of any kind. (2) They have no exact time of the births of gods. It means they have no real history of their imagined gods. (3) They have no scientific description of any kind regarding the creation and destruction of the world, or birth of souls and their *karmas* etc. (4) The number of their gods and goddesses is flexible. It means that during various periods of time new gods and goddesses have been created and added to the mythology. (5) There is no definite place or dimension for their gods to live in. Just some vague imaginations like the Greek gods are supposed to live on Mount Olympus in Greece. (6) There is absolutely no description of the Divineness of gods. (7) Their gods and goddesses are filled with human weaknesses like lust, greed, jealously and anger etc., and (8) their gods and goddesses have never been visualized in actual life because they are just the fiction stories of primitive minds. These are the common characteristics that are found in all the mythologies of the world. These mythologies assume the shape of the religion of that country and people keep on worshipping these imaginative figures for their whole life, just like Alexander worshipped Heracles and his mother worshipped Dionysus.

(3) The source of mythological imaginations.

If someone studies these mythologies carefully he will find that in spite of great descriptional differences there is some kind of basic similarity among them which makes one think that they might have come through some common source, and it is a fact that they did come from one common source.

All these mythologies describe about the creation of the world from the void or the sky. They also describe about the destruction of the world. They describe about the beginning of human civilization from some original couple like Adam and Eve. They also tell about gods and demons or evil spirits. Some mythologies (like that of Germanic people) tell about a huge 'world serpent' holding the earth, and about a certain distant land of happiness where good people go after death. Some mythologies tell about a certain region where all the dead people go, and so on. These are the general descriptions of the mythologies of the world. These descriptions are vague, bear no philosophical details and have no preciseness of the number of gods or goddesses or their living abodes etc., yet they have a general similarity. They also tell about the god of rain and thunder, god of fire, god of water, god of wisdom and god of arts etc.

As explained earlier on page 81, **the prime source from where these ideas originated was, of course, the stories of the Puranas of Bharatvarsh (India) which travelled through the trade routes from word of mouth and reached the other countries in a broken form** because they travelled from mouth to mouth. Then, from there, they travelled to other far-off countries of the world. As a general instinct, the primitive people also thought that certain invisible super forces might exist somewhere in the space which caused or controlled the natural happenings like disastrous rain, hail, strong thundering clouds, stormy wind or brush fire etc., which affected their daily life. When the stories of god of fire or god of rain and thunder etc. reached these people it supported their basic imaginations, and thus, all such stories of gods and goddesses that reached these places were incorporated in their folk tales with their added imaginations. In this way the mythologies started. They prevailed in the society for a long time. Later on, when the writing system started, they were written down in a book form. Thus, among the variations of the descriptions of the mythologies of different countries, there remains a similarity because the basic stories of creation, destruction, and gods and goddesses came from one single source, India (Bharatvarsh).

Mythological gods of Romans and Greeks.

(4) Western world knew only mythologies.

Before 2,000 years, when the world had a fair amount of population, the communication between the countries was extremely poor. There were only some trade connections between them. Even up to 200 years ago the communication system was very poor. The newspaper industry started in the early 19th century and national telephone communication systems started developing only at the end of the 19th century when the Bell telephone company spread its services to most of the major cities of the USA.

It has been explained earlier how the mythologies developed in the West through the trade connections, and, on that basis, how the religions of the world were formed. **Thus, from the very beginning, the western civilization knew only the mythologies and the mythological religions of their country.** Because of the lack of communication they could not receive the Divine truth of the Hindu scriptures which was in great detail; and when the communication systems developed, at that time the British were ruling India.

In this situation, when the people of the world know only mythological God and the dogmatic descriptions of their religious books, **it takes time and patience to understand the true reality of the supreme Divine God, His Divine abode, His Divine forms, His Divine Saints and Their Divine actions** which are described in the scriptures like the Upnishads, the Puranas, the Gita and the Brahm Sutra etc.

Had the world learned the real truth of Hindu scriptures which is Graciously gifted by God Himself for the good of

humankind, there would have been real and true 'God consciousness' in the world. The crime rate and the political exploitations in the world would have been much less than they are at present, and the scientific researches and the developments that are related to the evolution or creation of the cosmos (or any part of it) would have been going in the right direction because Hindu scriptures give the true guideline of the creation of the universe, creation of our earth planet and the sun, development of life on the earth planet, and the *karmic* and devotional destiny of the human beings.

Creator Brahma.

CHAPTER SIX

The misrepresentation of Hinduism.

(1) Bhartiya civilization after the destruction of the Mahabharat war, and the Harappan culture.

The Mahabharat war (3139 BC) had shattered the economy and abolished many localized civilizations of India. There were thousands of kings and millions of people who died in that war. That much loss of population in those days was a big thing, and, as a consequence of the war, big patches of uninhabited land stretched across the subcontinent. There were no common roads in those days to join two distant states of India, and thus, the communication between them was bleak. In that situation, the people, living in different locations of India, developed their own culture and their own communicating language which had classical or locally spoken Sanskrit background and the image of original Bhartiya civilization.

Time went on and gradually Brahmi script and Pali language developed in India. Pali language was liberally used to write the tenets of Buddhism. The prime Vedic civilization of Bharatvarsh would have been concentrated in Mathura, Allahabad and Varanasi areas which were always the center of Bhartiya culture and scriptural education.

People living around the Indus valley gradually developed their civilization. It was later on called the Harappan culture or Harappan civilization and was considered to exist around 2700-2500 BC. But it appears that that civilization was totally out of touch with the mainstream of Bhartiya culture, that's why their linguistic and literary developments remained in a very primitive shape. The inscriptions of Harappan civilization are found on seals and tablets in the form of signs which very much resemble Phoenician and Semitic signs that were developed around 1500 to 1000 BC and which became the prototype for the development of the writing systems of the western world.

But, on the other hand, we have the historical record, documented in the Bhagwatam itself (Bhag. Ma. 6/94, 95, 96) that in 3072 BC, 2872 BC and 2842 BC, three public programs of the recitation of the Bhagwatam and the discourses on Krishn leelas had happened in which Saints and the devotees participated.

We have thus two entirely different views about the civilization of India in almost the same period of time. To understand this situation I will give you an example: Suppose someone, who has never been to India and has only heard about it becomes curious and desires to see India. He and his younger brother in two helicopters approach India and prepare to land. One person lands near Bhabha Research Center (Bombay), interviews some people and talks to the research scientists of the Center and departs for his homeland. The other person loses the track and ends up landing in a jungle clearing where the tribal natives (called the *adivasis*) come to see the helicopter which is like a celestial machine for them. The person, baffled with the findings and unable to understand the tribal language, comes back home, disgusted and disappointed, where he finds his brother excitedly talking about all the good things of India. Both brothers tell their stories and both find it hard to believe each other. But both are facts, and both situations simultaneously exist.

It's an amazing fact that the Ganges Valley civilization is unbroken since 1900 million years. Thus, during the period of the Harappan culture, in some areas of **the Ganges valley, especially from Indraprasth (Delhi) and Mathura to Varanasi including Ayodhya and Allahbad,** India did have its advanced civilization because the revelation of the Bhagwatam (in 3072 BC) by Shukdeo was in Sanskrit language; and you should know that India is never bereft of such Sages and Saints who hold the knowledge of all the scriptures in their Divine mind.

When the historians write the history of India, even if they are sincere in their efforts, still they try to patch up the Harappan culture with Vedic culture and, in a worldly manner, they try to determine the advancement of the Sanskrit language which is eternally perfect. Such a notion is absolutely wrong. They think that they are trying to be logical in their historical research, but they forget this fact that *one cannot determine the history of Bharatvarsh on meager archaeological findings of coins, toys and pots.* Whereas the general history of Bharatvarsh is already written in its scriptures and the Puranas whose texts and the philosophical descriptions are the outcome of the Gracious and benevolent minds of eternal Saints.

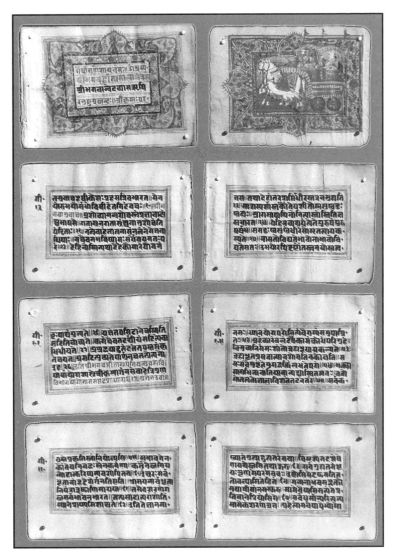

Handwritten ancient copy of the Gita

(2) The deliberate attempts of Sir William Jones to destroy the Divinity of Sanskrit language and the Bhartiya history.

It has already been explained that the Vedas, the Upnishads and the Puranas are: (a) eternal and Divine, (b) firstly produced by the creator Brahma, (c) they are not the writings of any human being, and (d) all of them were again revealed and rewritten by Bhagwan Ved Vyas long before he revealed the Bhagwatam, which was sometime before 3072 BC. Sanskrit language is also eternal which was firstly produced by Brahma and then it was reproduced by Ved Vyas along with the Vedas and the Upnishads.

But, the western writers and also the encyclopedias wrongfully say that the Sanskrit language started around 1500 BC and the Vedas came after that, whereas the Puranas came at a much later date sometime between 400 and 800 AD. They call Ved Vyas as only a legendary figure. Not only that, they derogate Bhartiya religion by all possible means, mutilate the history and abuse the Vedas by saying they are the poetic compositions of some foreign Aryan tribe who spoke Sanskrit and came to India from a still-unknown land around 1500 BC; and a lot more misleading statements like these.

For the last 200 years such a wrong image of Hinduism is being injected into the innocent minds of the school-going children as well as in the minds of the research scholars all over the world who study Hindu religion. Someone has to take the lead to correct these wrong statements about Bhartiya religion and history and feed the correct information into the

encyclopedias of the world and save millions of innocent seekers of truth whose spiritual progress is being hampered and paralyzed because of such negative informations that confuse their mind and damage their faith.

Let us now come to the reality and see how it all started. *On the 2nd of February, 1786,* a British jurist and a great scholar of Latin and Greek languages, Sir William Jones, who had also studied Sanskrit in India, gave a stunning speech in the Asiatic Society of Calcutta (Bengal) about the amazing similarity of some Sanskrit words with that of Latin and Greek, and the audience was thrilled with his skilled oratory and the style of the interpretation of his findings. But, in the end, he strongly asserted that, *not* Sanskrit, but there must be some other unknown common language from which all those languages must have originated.

Was he correct? *No. Absolutely not.* Because Sanskrit is the first language of the earth planet. Its root system of forming a word and its detailed grammar have no comparison with any of the languages of the world, and because it is the original language, so it is very likely that some of its daily spoken words could have been adopted by the other languages which itself is the evidence that Sanskrit is the mother language of the world.

But still his linguistic conjectures and skilled representation led the other European linguists to proceed on the same lines. Thus, the term **"Indo-European (or Proto-Indo-European) language" was created, which factually never existed.** *In this way, the attention of the whole world was withdrawn from looking into the greatness of the Sanskrit language and was drawn towards the opposite side of the truth, which was like searching for water in a mirage in a desert.*

❀❀❀

His other attempt to mutilate and to destroy the Divinity of Bhartiya history.

The statements of Jones and the fiction of Sandracottus.

Sir William Jones, President of the Asiatic Society of Bengal, gave his tenth anniversary discourse on February 28, 1793. The topic was, "Asiatic history, civil and natural," and it was published in the fourth volume of the Asiatic Researches, first printed in 1807, reprint 1979. This was his third attempt to destroy the culture and the history of Bharatvarsh by mutilating the historic dates.

Jones says in his speech,

"I cannot help mentioning a discovery which accident threw in my way, (I) thought my proofs must be reserved for an essay which I have destined for the fourth volume of your Transactions. To fix the situation of that Palibothra which was visited and described by Megasthenes, had always appeared a very difficult problem."

"…but this only difficulty was removed, when I found in *a classical Sanscrit book, near 2000 years old*, that Hiranyabahu, or golden-armed, which the Greeks changed into Erannoboas, or the river with a lovely murmur was in fact another name for the Son itself, though Megasthenes, from ignorance or inattention, has named them separately. This discovery led to another of greater moment; for *Chandragupta*, who, from a military adventurer, became, like Sandracottus, the sovereign of Upper Hindostan, actually fixed the seat of his empire at Patliputra, where he received ambassadors from foreign princes; *and was no other than that very Sandracottus* who concluded a treaty with Seleucus Nicator; so **that we have solved another problem,** to which we before alluded, and may in round numbers consider the *twelve and three hundredth years before Christ."* (pp. xxv to xxvii)

He tells in his speech that he has found a classical Sanskrit book of about 2,000 years old. The other thing he says is that Chandragupt Maurya was no other than the very Sandracottus who is described by Megasthenes to have made a treaty with Seleucus around 312 BC; and, to establish that *that* Chandragupt belonged to the Maurya dynasty, he mentions about some poem by Somdev which tells about the murder of Nand and his eight sons by Chandragupt in order to usurp the kingdom. In this way Jones created a fictitious connection between Chandragupt Maurya and Sandracottus. He says in his speech,

> "A most beautiful *poem by Somadev,* comprising a very long chain of instructive and agreeable stories, begins with the famed revolution at Patliputra, by the murder of King Nanda with his eight sons, and the usurpation of Chandragupta; and the same revolution is the subject of a tragedy in Sanscrit, entitled the Coronation of Chandra." (p. xxviii)

These were the basic points of his speech that was called the discovery of the identity of Chandragupt Maurya as Sandracottus.

Anyone could see that these people were adamantly prone to fabricating false statements all the time just to demean our culture and to destroy the genealogy of our religious history. **All the things referred to in this speech are absolutely wrong and outrageous.**

Finally, Somdev was just a story writer of fun and frolics. Yet he never described Chandragupt Maurya as the usurper of the kingdom and never connected him to the period of Seleucus Nicator and Alexander; and: **there was never a written book in India that lasted for 2,000 years, and there is no such statement in our religious writings to show that Chandragupt Maurya was in 312 BC.**

The scriptures, in ancient times, were written on *bhoj patra* (a paper thin bark of a Himalayan native tree) which never lasted in a readable condition for more than 500 to 800 years even with extreme care. These books were written for teaching and learning purposes so they were constantly in use (not like writing and hiding them in a cave as Dead Sea scrolls). When one book was worn out, another one was rewritten by the learned scholars under the guidance of the Master. Thus, the knowledge of the scriptures uninterruptedly continued. Now we know that there was no such book that was 2,000 years old. Moreover, Jones never produced or showed that book to anyone, even to his close associates. *It was simply his word of mouth to relate the fake story of a 2,000 year old book.*

As regards the period of King Chandragupt Maurya, the Puranas give a detailed genealogical account of all the kings of the Magadh kingdom, starting from the Mahabharat war (3139 BC) and up to the Andhra dynasty. Accordingly, the period of Chandragupt Maurya comes to the 1500's BC. **In no way could it be pushed forward to 312 BC. But those people (the British diplomats) were determined to do it that way because they wanted to squeeze the entire history of India within the time frame of their Aryan fiction story.**

Everyone who has read Megasthenes knows that his writings are most unreliable. But Jones found an excuse to quote the writings of Megasthenes where he describes the treaty of Seleucus with Sandracottus, the king of Magadh.

One thing we must mention, that there were two different dynasties that had similar names of their first king: the **Maurya dynasty** and **Gupt dynasty**. The first king of the Maurya dynasty, called **Chandragupt Maurya**, was in 1500's BC, and the first king of the Gupt dynasty, called **Chandragupt Vijayaditya**, was in 300's BC. The second king of Gupt dynasty and the son of Chandragupt Vijayaditya was Samudragupt Ashokaditya. He was the ruler of Magadh between 321 and 270 BC.

Chandragupt Maurya, who was the legitimate heir, was enthroned by a *brahman,* Chanakya. After cleverly killing Nand and his eight sons, Chanakya coronated him to the throne of Magadh. Chandragupt Maurya was not ambitious of conquering the other states of India and he did not receive foreign ambassadors because there were only trade relations of India with the foreign countries in those days (1500's BC) not political relations. So his kingdom was much smaller as compared to the kingdom of Chandragupt Vijayaditya of Gupt dynasty.

Chandragupt Vijayaditya, who was the son of Ghatotkach Gupt of Shreegupt Family, was made the commander-in-chief of the large army of Chandrashree of Andhra dynasty. After the accidental death of Chandrashree, his minor son, Prince Puloma, under the guardianship of Chandragupt, ruled for seven years. But Chandragupt finally terminated Puloma, *usurped the kingdom* and became the crowned king. In this way the kingship of Magadh was transferred from the Andhra dynasty to the Gupt dynasty. There were seven kings in the Gupt dynasty (called Abhir in the Bhagwatam) who ruled for 245 years between 328 to 83 BC. Chandragupt ruled from 328 to 321 BC and his son Samudragupt Ashokaditya from 321 to 270 BC. Chandragupt was an ambitious king. He invaded the neighboring states, conquered them and extended his kingdom up to Punjab. For his constant victories, he was titled *vijayaditya,* which means the sun of victory.

Thus, taking into account the above facts, it becomes clear that Sandracottus of Megasthenes could only be Samudragupt of Gupt dynasty, historically, and also according to the phonetic similarity of both of the names.

(1) It was Chandragupt, father of Samudragupt, who was a military adventurer and usurper of the kingdom, not Chandragupt Maurya who was made the king of Magadh in his young age by a brahman, Chanakya. (2) Chandragupt Maurya was in the 1500's BC, not 300's BC. (3) In the writings of Megasthenes the word "Maurya" was never used with the name of Sandracottus, and (4) there is absolutely no mention of Chanakya (Vishnugupt) who was the most important person in Chandragupt's life. These are such obvious evidences that no historian could deny them. But, Jones, deliberately overlooking these facts and taking an excuse of the unfounded writings of a disdained worldly person, Megasthenes, fabricated the story of matching Chandragupt Maurya with Sandracottus.

In fact, he was doing his job as he was told by his superiors. Now we can look into the statements of Megasthenes.

The non-credibility of the statements of Megasthenes.

The original writing of Megasthenes called 'Indica' has been lost. Extensive quotations from the writings of later Greek writers, Strabo, Diodorus and Arrian, still survive. Strabo was of the opinion that Megasthenes simply created *fables* and as such no faith could be placed in his writings. Strabo's own words: "Generally speaking the men who have written on the affairs of India were a set of liars. Deimachos is first, Megasthenes comes the next." Diodorus also held similar opinions about him.

Now see the personal situation of Megasthenes. He was a Greek, who had no understanding of Bhartiya language and culture, who knew only Greek mythology, who was appointed as an envoy to the court of Samudragupt in Patliputra (between 302 and 288 BC) so his activities were limited, who did not see much of India as he was mostly in Patliputra, and who was dependent on his translators to communicate with the people who were also ordinary folks. In this situation, how could he have learned about the Bhartiya culture and philosophy which is so extensive and deep, especially when he was dependent upon the incomplete information of his translators.

There may have been a "Proto-Germanic language" but there was never an "*Indo*-Iranian" family or a "Proto-*Indo*-European language." It was only a fiction that was created by Sir William Jones as it is evident from the development of the writing systems of the world (see pp. 89 to 102); and, the fact is, that Sanskrit language was always perfect since it was introduced in the world by the Rishis of Bharatvarsh and that's how its *apbhransh* are found in almost all the languages of the world.

Writing systems of the world.

The writing systems of the world developed in a very primitive style. First they were in a pictographic shape, then changed to a somewhat cursive form but with no vowels. Then, after a long time, it took the shape of a proper alphabet with vowels. In the beginning there were very few words to start with. The morphology gradually improved and the vocabulary expanded. The writing system of Sumerians and Egyptians died out, **Chinese** and **Semitic** survived which became the prototypes for the development of the writing systems of Eastern Asia and the rest of the world of today.

However, in all the alphabets of the languages of the world the basic characteristics of their vowel system resembles the vowels of the **Sanskrit** language along with some of the consonants also.

Sumerian: Pictographic 3500 BC
Cuneiform 3000-2000 BC
Sumerian Cuneiform (died out after the
Babylonian Cuneiform downfall of Babylonian
Assyrian Cuneiform empire in 323 BC)

Egyptian: Hieroglyphic 3000 BC
(Egyptian)
Hieratic 1100 BC
Demotic 700 BC (died out 400 AD)
Coptic 200 AD (died out 1500 AD)

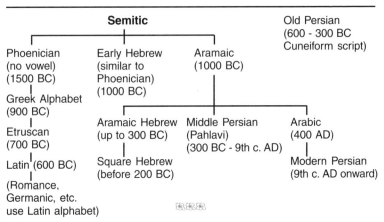

Semitic			Old Persian (600 - 300 BC Cuneiform script)
Phoenician (no vowel) (1500 BC)	Early Hebrew (similar to Phoenician) (1000 BC)	Aramaic (1000 BC)	
Greek Alphabet (900 BC)			
Etruscan (700 BC)	Aramaic Hebrew (up to 300 BC)	Middle Persian (Pahlavi) (300 BC - 9th c. AD)	Arabic (400 AD)
Latin (600 BC)	Square Hebrew (before 200 BC)		Modern Persian (9th c. AD onward)
(Romance, Germanic, etc. use Latin alphabet)			

(3) The fiction of Proto-Indo-European language, and Bopp.

Franz Bopp (1791-1867). He was a German linguist known for his works on tracing the phonetic laws of languages and researching the origin of the grammatical forms of the words of various languages. He was a professor of Oriental literature at the University of Berlin and introduced his first work "On the System of Conjugation of the Sanskrit…" in 1816. Working with **Colebrooke**, a close associate of **Sir William Jones** and an active member of the **Asiatic Society**, he translated Sanskrit manuscripts during his stay in London between 1816 and 1820. The *London Magazine* gave an excellent review of his works. He rejected the theories of the earlier linguists who held the view that Sanskrit is the original language of the world and followed the speculations of Mr. Jones. He published a Sanskrit and Latin glossary in 1830 and, between 1833 and 1852, he published his "Comparative Grammar of Sanskrit, Zend, Greek, Latin, Lithuanian, Old Slavic, Gothic and German." All of his works were on the line of theorizing the statement that Jones made in his Calcutta speech of 1786 to indicate that Sanskrit is not the first language of the world. **He was the main person who emphatically used and popularized the term 'Proto-Indo-European' or 'Indo-European' since 1833, and especially mentioned in his work the "Comparative Grammar…" Thus, coining of the term, "Proto-Indo-European language" was such a conspiracy that befooled the whole world (see chart p. 126).**

Working on the guidelines of Sir William Jones, Jacob Grim and Franz Bopp tried day and night for their whole life (for almost 50 years) to establish that not the Sanskrit but some unknown Proto-

Indo-European language was the first language of the world, but they failed. Because, all of their arguments regarding the change in the phonetic values of the alphabet and the words, spellings and the formation of words and of sentences etc. that occur in due course of time, are only related to all those languages of the world which didn't have even proper alphabet and vowels in the very beginning. One should understand that Sanskrit was absolutely perfect since its appearance in the world whereas all other languages of the world developed from scratch.

The deliberate creation of the term "Proto-Indo-European language" and the unequalled uniqueness of Sanskrit morphology.

It is an open fact that the phonology (the speech sound) and morphology (the science of word formation) of the Sanskrit language is entirely different from all of the languages of the world. There is no comparison in any way.

1. The sound of each of the 36 consonants and the 16 vowels of Sanskrit are fixed and precise since the very beginning. It was never changed, altered, improved or modified. So all the words of the Sanskrit language always had the same pronunciation as they have today.

2. Its morphology or word formation is unique and of its own kind where a word is formed from a tiny seed root (called *dhatu*) in a precise grammatical order which has been the same since the very beginning.

3. There has never been any kind, class or nature of change in the science of the Sanskrit grammar as it is seen in other languages of the world as they passed through one stage to another.

4. The perfect form of the Vedic Sanskrit language had already existed thousands of years earlier even before the infancy of the earliest prime languages of the world like Greek, Hebrew and Latin etc.

5. When a language is spoken by unqualified people the pronunciation of the word changes to some extent; and when these words travel by word of mouth to another region of the land, with the gap of some generations, it permanently changes its form and shape to some extent. Just like the Sanskrit word *matri*, with a long 'a' and soft 't,' became *mater* in Greek and *mother* in English. The last two words are called the *'apbhransh'* of the original Sanskrit word *'matri.'* Such *apbhranshas* of Sanskrit words are found in all the languages of the world and this situation itself proves that Sanskrit was the mother language of the world.

Now I will give you one example of a famous verse from the very ancient literature, the Vedas.

"अन्धं तमः प्रविशन्ति येऽविद्यामुपासते ।" (यजुर्वेद ४०/९)

It means, "Those who are the worshippers of only materialism enter into darkness." In this sentence *yah* (those) and *vishanti* (enter) are the pronoun and the main verb. The word *vishanti* is formed of the root word (*dhatu*) *vish*. These word formations of nouns, pronouns and verbs were always in perfect grammatical form since thousands and thousands of years and they are still the same without any change, and will remain the same in future. A person living in Iceland or New Zealand, if he knows the Sanskrit language, he will use the same words because there is no change of dialect or inflection in Sanskrit language. **Time and space make no difference in the representation of Sanskrit language.**

Considering all the five points as explained above and seeing the example of the ancient Vedic verse, it is quite evident that Sanskrit was the first and the original language of the world; and the western linguists of the earlier times also believed in this fact. It is so obvious that anyone who learns Sanskrit grammar knows these facts. But still, these 18th and 19th century linguists created a term 'Proto-Indo-European' for the original parent language which was assumed to be spoken about 5,000 years ago by the nomads who assumingly roamed around near the southeast European plains. They further assumed that from the speech of those earlier nomads came the languages of the world like Greek, Latin, Slavic, Russian, Germanic and Indo-Iranian etc., whereas the Sanskrit language came from the Indo-Iranian group.

Now the question is, when an original parent language, Sanskrit, is already in existence, why was the 'Proto-Indo-European' term designed, and, instead of deriving the ancestral relationship of the languages of the world from the Sanskrit language through the findings of the Sanskrit *apbhransh* in them, why was an inferior parallelism made of the Sanskrit language with the Greek and Latin languages?

Although the fact was that certain daily usable words and the numerals like *trya, sapt, panch* (three, seven, five), and the religious stories of India travelled to the Middle East and to Greece and were adopted in their language and culture, that's how certain Sanskrit *apbhransh* words were found in Greek, its descendent Latin and the Germanic languages. But this fact was altered and mutilated by vigorously constructing extensive arguments of their own choice, not by one or two linguists, but by a number of well known linguists, and that also for **84 years of day and night efforts from Jones (1786) to Neogrammarians (1870)** including Jacob, Grimm and Franz Bopp.

Isn't it laughable? Why did they do so and create such a monstrous lie that confused and misled the sincere intelligentsia of the whole world? It was only the follow up of the diplomatic scheme of Jones to demean the Sanskrit language.

Now we should know that apart from the Sanskrit language there is no such thing as Proto-Indo-European language as it is self-evident from the findings of Sanskrit apbhransh words in all the existing Asian and European languages.

❀❀❀

(4) The fiction of Aryan invasion, introduction of English language, suppression of Sanskrit language, and a well organized scheme to mutilate the history and the Divine greatness of Bharatvarsh.

The preplanned scheme of Jones to introduce the idea that Sanskrit was an outside language gave birth to the speculation of the imagined existence of some Central Asian (Aryan) race who spoke Sanskrit and who brought Sanskrit language to India when they forcefully entered the country. In this way, **the fiction of the Aryan invasion was created much later, sometime in the 1800's** by the same group of people and was extensively promoted by Max Müller. Let us now probe into the matter and see how this story was formulated.

It is a well known fact that India is called Aryavart. Manu Smriti (2/21, 22) describes the exact location of Aryavart which lies from the south of the Himalayas and all the way up to the Indian ocean. Its inhabitants are called the Arya. But it is not a locally spoken name. Commonly, we write Bharatvarsh for India in general and scriptural writings. The territory of India (or Bharatvarsh or Aryavart) during the Mahabharat war (3139 BC) was up to Iran. So the ancient Iranian people also used to call themselves the Aryans.

People of the British regime using this information, fabricated a story that some unknown race of Central Asia who came and settled in Iran were called the Aryans and they were Sanskrit speaking people. They invaded India, established themselves

141

permanently, and wrote the Vedas. Those who introduced this ideology never cared to produce any evidence in support of their statement because it never existed, and furthermore, fiction stories don't need evidences as they are self-created dogmas.

If someone carefully looks into the ancient history of India, he will find that there was no such thing as an Aryan invasion. Since the very beginning of human civilization, Hindus (Aryans) are the inhabitants of Bharatvarsh (India) which is called Aryavart. In the Bhartiya history there are descriptions of Shak and Hun invasions and also of Muslim invasions but never an Aryan invasion. It was simply a figment of the imagination of the British diplomats that fabricated this false story. However, after creating this story, they had to fix the period of the entry of the Aryans into India which needed a careful decision.

The second millennium BC was the period of migration and the expansion of major civilizations in the Middle East area. The **Sumerians** were at their peak around 2000 BC, the **Babylonians** were expanding their empire around 1700 BC and the **Assyrians** established their independent kingdom around 1400 BC. The **Hittite empire** (Turkey) also flourished during the second millennium BC. The Hittite language used Akkadian cuneiform script of which the earliest known record of cuneiform text goes back to 1700 BC. The cursive form of the alphabetical writing of **early Hebrew** and **Aramaic** languages started taking their first primitive shape around 1000 BC, and the **Greek** around 900 BC.

Considering these factors of social and literal developments in the Middle East, they randomly fixed the fifteenth century BC for their speculated Aryan invaders, telling that they came from the Iranian side, forcefully entered the Indus valley, settled there and spread towards the south.

This is the whole story about the Aryan invasion fiction which was so extensively popularized that it appeared in the writings of every historian.

Max Müller promoted this invasion story and formulated his dates of Vedic origin accordingly.

In **1833, Thomas B. Macaulay** (1800-1859) was appointed to the Governor General's supreme council by the East India Company to modify the education system of India. Discouraging Sanskrit education he designed a western style of English education that was supposed to *'produce such a group of people who would be Indian in blood and color, but English in taste, opinion and intellect.'*

In October **1844, Lord Hardings**, Governor General for India, passed a resolution that all government appointments in India should have a preference to the English knowing people. This condition hampered the Indian culture and greatly promoted English education in India.

爨爨爨

A well organized scheme to mutilate the history and the Divine greatness of Bharatvarsh*

The very first issue (1784) sponsored by the Asiatic Society of Bengal contains a long essay (of 47 pages) by its President, Sir William Jones in which, by all means, he demeans and abuses all the forms of God and Goddess of Bhartiya religion saying that he was *"drawing a parallel between the Gods of the Indian and European Heathens."* (Asiatic Researches, p. 190)

It was all done according to the secret planning of the British diplomats in a well organized manner where they wanted to: (1) Degrade the Hindu religion to their utmost and to show that it is no better than the (mythological) religions of Greece and ancient Italy; and (2) to perfectly mutilate the Bhartiya history and its Divinity by creating a fiction of Aryan invasion.

If we look to their doings, during the period they ruled India, with this angle of view, everything becomes crystal clear.

---

*Detailed descriptions of all these issues with positive evidences are in "The True History and the Religion of India"

143

(A brief review of their working.)

1784 • In January 1784, the Asiatic Society of Bengal was established in Calcutta under the patronage of Warren Hastings and Sir William Jones was appointed its President. Its secret aim was to find ways of how to accomplish their hidden objectives mentioned above. Its literary works were published in the name of "Asiatic Researches."

1784 • Towards the end of 1784 Jones produced his first essay (described above) which was the first most important work of the Asiatic Researches.

1786 • On 2nd February 1786, Jones, in his Presidential speech, produced his new fabricated theory of some unknown *proto language* that was designed to disprove the authenticity of the Sanskrit language.

1793 • Jones in his 10th Presidential speech discredits our entire history as described in the Puranas and places Chandragupt Maurya as the contemporary of Alexander.

1796 • Jones, trying to defame Hindu religion in an absurd way (telling that *Vedic Rishis loved to eat meat*), arranged to have a manuscript of Manu Smriti that was fabricated with the statements of meat eating. He translated it verse by verse, titling it "Hindu Law or the Ordinances of Manu," and mentioning that they are *'the words of the Most High'* for the Hindus. Similar fabrications (including the mutilations of the dynastic dates of the kings of Magadh) were also done in other scriptures, like the Puranas and Grihya Sutras etc. **Such ingenious trickeries befooled the whole world and even the sincere Hindu writers.**

1828 • All the articles of the Asiatic Researches including the writings of its secretary Mr. H.H. Wilson were purposely designed to be extremely derogatory.

1832 • Mr. Wilson publishes his translation of Vishnu Puran in which he uses all the derogatory words, which he knew, to demean the Puranas and the Sages and Saints. He also details the discrepancies in the dates of the kings of Magadh that appear in the verses of the Puranas. *Evidences show that these discrepancies were fabricated in the Puranas by those people themselves.**

1847 • Max Müller was appointed by the East India Company to wrongly translate the theme of the Vedas.

1852 • Jones died in 1794 but in 8 years he could not produce the full thesis of his created theory of some unknown *protolanguage*. Another coworker of the Asiatic Researches group of people, Franz Bopp worked hard for his whole life and then produced his detailed work around 1852 to substantiate the ideology of Proto-Indo-European language which Jones had created (but, in fact, all of his arguments were baseless).

Planning of their scheme.

They decided to: (1) fix the period of the Vedas around 1500 BC; (2) call Hindu scriptures the myths of primitive heathens; (3) demean all the Vedic Sages to their utmost (calling the Vedic rituals

---

*It's a proven fact that the rulers of India of those days had a strong *motive* and full *opportunity* to procure, mutilate, fabricate and destroy the unwanted handwritten scriptures. Jones tried to crush the historic dates in his speech of 1793 and Mr. Wilson produced his translation in 1832. There was a gap of 39 years which was good enough time to do whatever they wanted. The verses of Matsya Puran are themselves the most important evidence where they give the names and say that 6 kings of Maurya dynasty ruled for 199 (6 + 70 + 36 + 8 + 9 + 70) years. Immediately after that, the last verse says that 10 kings ruled for 137 years. *This statement itself proves that these lines are the fabricated ones because it could not be a copying mistake.* You cannot find such a copying-scholar who could not recognize the difference between the figures 6 and 10, and 199 and 137. *Except for a few verses in only a few Puranas (specially Vayu, Matsya and Vishnu) that relate to the kings of Magadh*, the rest of the descriptions telling the entire history of Bharatvarsh along with its related events and names and all the 'creation' dates of *yugas* and *manvantars* etc. (which are in trillions of years) in all the 18 Puranas are in an exacting manner. Why? Because only those few verses about the kings of Magadh were fabricated.

as *brahmanism*); (4) establish Chandragupt Maurya as the contemporary of Alexander; and a lot more.

For the execution of their plan, they: (a) appointed, employed and influenced a selected group of people who extensively wrote books on Indian culture, society, history and religion exactly as they had planned; (b) procured all the Sanskrit manuscripts as much as they could, kept whatever they wanted, adulterated the historic facts of some of them and destroyed the rest of the manuscripts and books because they conflicted with their plans, (c) destroyed all the ancient history books wherever they found them; (d) employed a great scholar of Calcutta Sanskrit College in 1866 to incorporate the derogative meaning of certain Vedic words in the prime Sanskrit dictionary; (e) wrote the most derogatory articles about Hinduism in the Encyclopedic Britannica of 1856; (f) fabricated certain sections of the Bhavishya Puran and other Vedic ritualistic scriptures like the Grihya Sutras etc.; (g) may have also fabricated the descriptions of the kings of Magadh in the Puranas; (h) (circumstantial evidences show that they) destroyed the most important research manuscripts of a great Indian scholar sometime after 1917; (i) created false synchronizations of the edicts and the coins; and so on.

From the above description you can assume how badly Hinduism was mutilated by the rulers of India for hundreds of years and was misrepresented in the world. *Thousands and thousands of such derogatory books and magazines were published by them which are still flooding the libraries of the whole world and give an entirely wrong image of Hinduism.*

CHAPTER SEVEN

The derogatory views of western writers and their adoption by Hindu scholars.

(1) Max Müller. A paid employee, who translated the Rigved in a demeaning style. The hidden secrets of his life.

(1) Max Müller was a British agent, especially employed (in 1847) to write the translations of the Vedas in such a demeaning way so that the Hindus should lose faith in them. His personal letter to his wife dated December 9, 1867 reveals this fact.

(2) He was highly paid for this job. According to the statistical information given on page 214 of the "English Education, 1798-1902" by John William Adamson, printed by Cambridge University Press in 1930, the revised scale of a male teacher was £90 per year and for a woman, £60 in 1853. The present salary of a lecturer in London is £14,000 to £36,000 per year, which averages a minimum of at least 200 times increase in the last 146 years. Max Müller was paid £4 per sheet of his writing which comes to **£800** of today (1999). This is an incredibly high price **for only one sheet of writing.** But it's the general law of business, that the price of a commodity increases with its demand. The British were in such an

imperative need to get someone to do this job and Max Müller was the right person, so they paid whatever Max Müller asked for. His enthusiastic letter to his mother dated April 15, 1847 reveals this fact.

(3) Max Müller's letters dated August 25, 1856 and December 16, 1868 reveal the fact that he was desperate to bring Christianity into India so that the religion of the Hindus would be doomed.

His letters also reveal that:

(4) He lived in poverty before he was employed by the British, and (5) in London, where he lived, there were a lot of orientalists working for the British.

Letters of Max Müller.

"The Life and Letters of Friedrich Max Müller." First published in 1902 (London and N.Y.). Reprint in 1976 (USA).

1. To his wife, Oxford, *December 9, 1867.*

"...I feel convinced, though I shall not live to it, that this edition of mine and the translation of the Veda will hereafter tell to a great extent on the fate of India, and on the growth of millions of souls in that country. It is the root of their religion, and to show them what that root is, I feel sure, the only way of uprooting all that has sprung from it during the last 3,000 years."

2. To his mother, Lincoln's Inn Fields, *April 15, 1847.*

"I can yet hardly believe that I have at last got what I have struggled for so long... I am to hand over to the Company, ready for press, fifty sheets each year; for this I have asked £200 a year, £4 a sheet. They have been considering the matter since December, and it was only yesterday that it was officially settled."

"...In fact, I spent a delightful time, and when I reached London yesterday I found all settled, and I could say and feel, Thank

God! Now I must at once send my thanks, and **set to work to
earn the first £100**."

3. To Chevalier Bunsen. 55 St. John Street, Oxford, *August 25, 1856.*

"**India is much riper for Christianity than Rome or Greece
were at the time of St. Paul.** The rotten tree has for some time
had artificial supports… For **the good of this struggle I should
like to lay down my life, or at least to lend my hand to bring
about this struggle.** Dhulip Singh is much at Court, and is
evidently destined to play a political part in India."

To the duke of Argyll. Oxford, *December 16, 1868.*

"India has been conquered once, but India must be conquered
again, and that second conquest should be a conquest by
education. Much has been done for education of late, but **if the
funds were tripled and quadrupled,** that would hardly be
enough… **A new national literature may spring up,
impregnated with western ideas...** As to religion, that will
take care of itself. The missionaries have done far more than
they themselves seem to be aware of."

"The ancient religion of India is doomed, and if Christianity
does not step in, whose fault will it be?"

4. To his mother. Paris, *December 23, 1845.*

"**…instead of taking money from you, my dearest mother, I
could have given you some little pleasure. But it was
impossible, unless I sacrificed my whole future…** I have again
had to get 200 francs from Lederhose, and with the money you
have just sent shall manage till January or February."

5. To his mother. *September 1, 1847.*

"My rooms in London are delightful. In the same house lives
Dr. Trithen, an orientalist, whom I knew in Paris, and who was

once employed in the Office for Foreign Affairs in St. Petersburg. Then there are a great many other orientalists in London, who are mostly living near me, and we form an oriental colony from all parts of the world... We have a good deal of fun at our cosmopolitan tea-evenings."

Writings of Max Müller.

See a few specimens of his writings:

- The Vedas are like the twaddles of idiots and the ravings of madmen. Their downright absurdity can hardly be matched anywhere... (A History of Ancient Sanskrit Literature, Ch. II, p. 389)

- The Vedas are intended from the beginning for an uncivilized race of mere heathens and savages... (The Vedas, Ch. II, p. 12)

- Sanskrit and English are the varieties of one and the same language... (Ch. II, p. 13)

- Sacrifice was a natural occupation for the Vedic savages... (Ch. III, p. 55)

- That Vishnu in India, became in time, an independent deity as Apollo and Dionysus were in Greece. (Ch. III, p. 74)

- The Greek and Indian gods were not beings that ever existed... (Ch. III, p. 64)

That was Friedrich Max Müller who many Hindu scholars appreciate.

(2) F. E. Pargiter (1852-1927).

I.C.S. (Indian Civil Service), High Court Judge, Calcutta. Retired 1906, Vice President of the Asiatic Society, London.

Pargiter writes in:
"Ancient Indian Historical Tradition."

- The whole of the Sanskrit literature has no historical works. (Chapter 1, page 2)

- Aryans established themselves in India through long warfare. (1/3)

- Vedic literature does not give any information who compiled them… No trust can be placed in the Vedic literature as regards any matter which the *brahmans* found. (1/9,10)

- The original *brahmans* were not so much priests… they were wizards… (26/308)

- These statements of *yugas* and *manvantar* are generally worthless for chronological purposes. (15/178)

- Chandragupt began to reign in or about 322 BC. He was preceded by the Nine Nandas… The reign of Nandas would be 80 years. (15/179)

- From the Bharat battle to the Mahapadm (Nand) there were 37 Magadh kings… the total of all of their reigns (according to Puran) is (940 + 138 + 330) = 1,408 years. These figures cannot be relied upon. (These figures according to the Bhagwatam are 1,000 + 138 + 360 = 1,498 years.)

- The reign of Mahapadm (Nand) began in 402 BC (322 + 80) by overthrowing the last king of Shishunag dynasty.

- From the 7th king of Brihadrath dynasty and up to the last king of Shishunag dynasty, the reigning period was 448 years; and from the 1st to 6th king of Brihadrath dynasty (the first dynasty after Mahabharat war), the reigning period was 100 years.

- Thus (402 + 448 + 100) 950 BC is the date of Mahabharat battle. (15/179 to 182)

"The Purana Text of the Dynasties of the Kali Age."

- The Puranas were originally in *prakrit* (local) language. What we have now is the Sanskritized version of older *prakrit shlokas*.

- The Bhavishya Puran existed in the 3rd century AD and Matsya Puran borrowed what the Bhavishya contained before the Gupt era (320 AD). Then Vayu, Brahmand and Vishnu Puran were compiled accordingly.

- The *brahmans* fabricated the passages, and the later readers of the Puranas further fabricated the details of the text.

- The *brahmans* converted *prakrit* words of the Puranas into Sanskrit and substituted future tense for past tenses... and altered them to the form of a prophecy uttered by Ved Vyas. (Intro, p. 10 to 27)

Comments. Every Hindu, who has some understanding about the Bhagwatam and the Gita, knows that all of the Vedas and the Puranas were written by the descended Divine Personality Ved Vyas in Sanskrit language, and Mahabharat war had happened before *kaliyug* started. Also, every educated person who has consulted the yearly **Kashi Hindu Vishvavidyalaya** calendar, called the Panchang, which is a reputed calendar of India, knows that over 5,000 years have passed since *kaliyug* started because **the calendar itself gives the exact year of the start of kaliyug which comes to 3102 BC.**

The Mahabharat war: 3139 BC is the date that is recognized by all of the *acharyas*, *Jagadgurus* and the Divine Masters. But, Pargiter, rejecting all those evidences, assumes a date 950 BC in his mind and, squeezing the reigning period of all the dynasties that ruled Magadh, he just terminates 2,189 years out of his free will and says that Mahabharat war happened in 950 BC.

The Bhagwatam says that the four dynasties, 21 kings of Brihadrath, 5 of Pradyot, 10 of Shishunag and Mahapadm Nand Family ruled for 1,598 years (1,000 + 138 + 360 + 100). So, 3139 BC (-) 1,598 years of the total reign of four dynasties comes to 1541 BC, which was the coronation year of Chandragupt Maurya who succeeded after Mahapadm Nand.

Instead of 1541 BC, Pargiter took 322 BC for Chandragupt Maurya because it was stated by Sir William Jones, and thus, terminated 1,219 years in one shot. Then he reduced 970 years more from the total reigning period of the four dynasties (1,000 + 138 + 360 + 100 = 1,598). He took only 628 years instead of 1,598 years, and thus, fabricated a round figure of (322 BC + 628) 950 years BC.

It is quite amusing how he arrived at the 628 year figure. Pargiter gave **80** years to Mahapadm and his sons, the last of the four dynasties. Then he gave **448** years to the 31 kings of the first three dynasties (at the rate of 14.45 years per king), starting from Sanjit, the seventh king of the Brihadrath dynasty, and up to the last king of Shishunag dynasty. Then he gave the remaining **100** years to the first 6 kings of Brihadrath dynasty which were left out. Thus, he completed the figure of 628 years; 80 + 448 + 100 = 628. (He counted 22 kings of Brihadrath dynasty, 5 of Pradyot and 10 of Shishunag dynasty.)

Showing his intellectual skills he gives an extensive argument telling that the reigning period of the kings according to the Puranas seemed too long to him so he reduced them. Isn't it ridiculous, that the reigning period of our historical kings is at the mercy of Pargiter which he may reduce at any time according to his whim. To be more practical, why didn't he argue with his Queen Victoria to resign immediately from her Queenship as she was already over-reigning? (Pargiter was in the judicial services during the period of Queen Victoria who reigned for 64 years.)

Thus, it is evident that the writings of F. E. Pargiter were also the exploitations of British diplomacy. There were a number of writers who were working on the same lines and were in some way associated with the Asiatic Society of Bengal (Calcutta), established by **Warren Hastings** and **Sir William Jones**.

We are giving a few names of such writers: **J. Petersen, F. Wilford, Henry Thomas Colebrooke, Horace Hayman Wilson, Franz Bopp, Theodore Goldstucker, Vincent Smith, Hermann Georg Jacobi, Arthur Anthony Macdonnel, Richard Karl von Garbe, Edward Washburn Hopkins, Moris Winternitz, Arthur Berriedale Keith,** etc.

(3) The effect of western writers on Hindu scholars.

The primacy of English education and the abundance of biased literature regarding the history and the Vedic religion affected the Hindu society a great deal. The wrong historical dates of Hindu dynasties and the notable personalities that they fixed, especially **Buddh**, **Chandragupt** and **Ashok**, became a guideline, and many Hindu writers followed the same wrong trend.

Certain great scholars and the so-called patriots of India also had profound effects of western education on their minds that held the feeling of lowness for Hindu culture, history and religion. They too collected the intellectual dirt of the western writers and used it in their writings.

Not knowing what were they doing, their writings like: "Ram was only a good man. He was not God," betrayed and confused millions of Hindus and contempted the authentic writings of Ved Vyas which are the national treasures of India.

We will give you some examples.

S. Radhakrishnan (1888-1975).

His brief biography: Born near Madras, South India, Sarvepalli Radhakrishnan showed his intelligence since childhood. He received a Master's degree in Arts from Madras University. His essay on "Ethics of the Vedant" (as a partial fulfillment for his Master's degree) was highly appreciated by professor A.G. Hogg as it contained the boldness of thought and the neglect for the personal form of God.

In 1909 he was appointed to the Department of Philosophy of the Madras Presidency College. In 1918 he was appointed as a professor of Philosophy at the University of Mysore and in 1921 he was appointed at the University of Calcutta. In 1926 he represented the University of Calcutta at the Congress of the Universities of the British Empire. From 1936 to 1939 he was appointed as a professor of Eastern Religions and Ethics at Oxford University, in 1939 he was elected as 'Fellow of the British Academy', and from 1939 to 1948 he was Vice Chancellor of the Benares Hindu University. He was the Vice President of India from 1952 to 1962 and he also held the Office of the Chancellor, Delhi University from 1953 to 1962. In 1962 he was elected the President of India.

The derogative views of Radhakrishnan about Hindu religion and scriptures.

We have written about Jones and Max Müller. Radhakrishnan was not only their admirer, he was the promoter of their views which is clearly evident from his writings. His prejudicial attitude toward the Vedic religion and sneering opinions about the historical Divine Masters and their writings are seen in every book he wrote. See a few examples:

Indian Philosophy Vol. I, first print 1923, reprint 1996. **Indian Philosophy Vol. II,** first print 1927, reprint 1996. **The Bhagavadgita** first print 1948, reprint 1994. **The Principal Upanisads** first print 1953, reprint 1995.

See a few examples:

(About the early Hindus of Vedic religion)

"Man's never-ceasing effort to raise himself **above the level of the beast** to a moral and spiritual height finds a striking illustration in India." (Indian Philosophy Vol. II, p. 766)

(About the Rigved)

**"The process of god-making in the factory of man's mind
cannot be seen so clearly anywhere else as in the Rg-
Veda."** (Indian Philosophy Vol. I, p. 73)

(About the Atharvaved)

"The religion of the Atharva-Veda is that of the primitive
man, to whom the world is full of shapeless ghosts and
spirits of death... The terrific powers could only be appeased
by bloody sacrifices, human and animal... The religion of
the Atharva-Veda is an amalgam of Aryan and non-Aryan
ideals." (Vol. I, pp. 119, 120)

(About the Upnishads)

**"The Upanisads contain the earliest records of Indian
speculation...** they contain much that is inconsistent and
unscientific." (Vol I, p. 138)

(About the Puranas)

"The Puranas are the religious poetry of the period of the
schools, representing through **myth and story, symbol and
parable,** the traditional view of God and man... They were
composed with the purpose of undermining, if possible, **the
heretical doctrines of the times."** (Vol. II, p. 663)

(About Chaitanya Mahaprabhu and his disciples)

"The orthodox were much disturbed by his startling ways.
He accepted converts from Islam freely... His **disciples, Rupa
and Sanatana, were renegade converts to Islam and
outcasts from the Hindu society."** (Vol. II, p. 761)

The writer of the "Indian Philosophy," Radhakrishnan, calls
the early Hindus '*the beast*' and the Divine wisdom of the Rishis
'*the god-making factory,*' and defines the **Vedic religion** as '*the
religion of the primitive man in the world of ghosts and goblins
who were only satisfied with bloody sacrifices.*' He speaks of the

teachings of the Upnishads and the Puranas as '*speculation, myth, parables and heretical doctrines*' and criticizes the Brahm Sutra.

No true Hindu can utter such words for our Divine scriptures and the Vedic religion. They are all *tamoguni* writings.

⁂

His wiliness, antipathy towards our *acharyas* and his inclination towards Christianity.

Radhakrishnan criticizes Chaitanya Mahaprabhu who is the most adorable figure to millions of Hindus, and degrades the most respected *rasik* Saints of Vrindaban, Roop and Sanatan Goswami, by calling them '*renegade converts to Islam and the outcasts from the Hindu society.*'

He doesn't stop over there. **To justify the Aryan invasion fiction, he condemns the entire history of all the manvantars by telling that 'Indian civilization is about 4,000 years old'** in Volume I, page 46, of his book the "Indian Philosophy"; and in Volume II, page 656, he draws a parallel between the description of God (*brahm*) of the Upnishads with the description of God in the Jewish and Christian religious book (the Bible).

It may be shocking for some people to know that the world renowned philosopher, bearing the prestige of having the seat of Vice President and the President of India for many years, had a leaning towards the western Christian faith and had anti-Vedic thoughts in his head, which he covered behind the big turban that showed the sign of Hinduism. But the fact is, that his own statements are the evidences of his own duplicitous character, when he writes,

> "**To love God is to take up the cross.** The surrender of the soul to the heavenly Bridegroom... a metaphor not peculiar to India." (Vol. I, p. 495)

> "To take up the cross" is a pure Christian saying which means to do everything for the sake of Christianity. But

158

taking the example of a general Christian proverb and befitting it with the occasion of *maharas* and with the unlimited depth of *Gopis'* love for Krishn whose Divine sweetness surpassed all the forms of Divine Blissfulness, positively expresses the total anglicization of Radhakrishnan's mind.

In the Indian Philosophy Vol. I, page 103, he writes,

"The personal God brooding over the waters **the Narayana resting on the eternal Ananta. It is the god of Genesis** who says, *Let there be, and there was*."

Here again Radhakrishnan compares the Divine greatness of Gracious and kind God Narain (Vishnu) with the wrathful God of the Old Testament (Genesis).

🙙🙚🙙🙚

The reason of his being famous as an Indian philosopher.

There were two reasons: (a) His political status as the President of India, and (b) the ignorance of the common people about the quality of his writings. Hindus have tremendous faith in the Gita, Bhagwat, Ramayan and the Upnishads etc. Just the thought, that Radhakrishnan had translated *the Gita and the Upnishads*, gave an air of respect to him. Moreover, in the political field, he was well known to Indians as being a good politician, and people had a regard for him. His oratory was well known, and his presentation of a subject before the students was promising. All these things promoted his name. His appointment to the Oxford University as a Professor of Philosophy gave him a further rise, and his political distinction promulgated his fame when he became the President of India. The notion, that 'the President of India' had written books on Indian philosophy and translated the Gita, augmented his fame as a philosopher, and thus, he came to be known as a world figure in philosophy.

But, it was all in the air. Had the Indians in common known what really he had written about the Rishis, the Vedas, Bhartiya scriptures, our most revered *acharyas* and Saints and about the Divine descensions, Bhagwan Ram and Krishn, the story would have been entirely different.

More than ninety-five percent of the Indian population reads the scriptures that are published in Indian languages, so they remain unaware of the biasness of his writings (which were written in English only). Very few who take higher education in the Indian philosophy and religion happen to study such books as those of Radhakrishnan and other similar Indian or European writers. By the time they finish their course they accumulate so much philosophical confusion in their mind by studying the works of worldly and incompetent writers that most of them lose faith in the devotional aspects of Hindu religion and develop a kind of no-regard feeling for the Divinity of the scriptures, *Jagadgurus* and the great historical Masters as well. Thus, it doesn't matter to them what Radhakrishnan or any other writer has written about the religion, philosophy or the culture of India.

Many people who regarded Radhakrishnan as a philosopher have simply praised him without even knowing what he has actually written in his books. Moreover, no one has ever written genuine comments on his writings. **So, the dark side of his writings always remained hidden, and that was a plus point on his part that maintained his image as a great Indian philosopher.**

The writings of Radhakrishnan were more damaging to Bhartiya religion as compared to the European writers.

The derogatory writings of the western scholars, as initiated by the British, left a great impact on the Indian minds. But the reconfirmation of those western views by Radhakrishnan had much more damaging effects and confused millions of scholars of philosophy and religion around the world by giving them entirely wrong input about Hindu philosophy, Hindu scriptures and the Hindu religion. Just examine some of his writings.

Extracts from the **Indian Philosophy Vol. I & II** (IP/I,II) and the **Principal Upanishads** (PU).

- Rigved has the impassionate utterances of the primitive poetic souls. (IP/I-71)

- Atharvaved contains the pre-Vedic animist religion of spirits and ghosts. It gives an idea of demonology prevalent in the tribes of India. (PU-45;IP/I-121)

- The earliest Vedic seers worshipped nature... the **Vedic gods were stupidly self-centered... gods and ghosts governed the life of people.** (IP/I-121)

- The Upnishads (*aranyakas*) are the speculations of the hermits. Their teachings are lost in the jumbled chaos of puerile superstition. (IP/I-355)

- **He (Radhakrishnan) cannot accept Krishn of the Puranas. It was only the unknown author of the Gita who made Krishn famous through his writings and devised him to pose as God (brahm).** (IP/I-496, 521)

- **Ram was only a good man. He was not God.** His religion is polytheistic and external.

- In the Chaitanya religion the ultimate reality is Vishnu, and there is nothing much in their theory (*achintya bhedabhed vad*). (IP/II-761)

You can see that Radhakrishnan, introducing his skeptical views, despises the Divineness of the philosophy and the religion of Bharatvarsh.

He calls the *Vedic Rishis as primitive poets whose impassionate utterances are the Rigved. He says that Atharvaved incorporates the demonology of primitive tribes; Vedic gods are stupidly self-centered; and the Upnishads are childish superstitions.*

He criticizes the Divinity of Krishn, and says that (Bhagwan) *Ram was only a good man, not God.* He condemns the Divine greatness of Vaikunth by calling it the imagined heaven of Ramanujacharya (IP/II-711). He refutes the most impressive theory of the Vaishnavas of Vrindaban, the *achintya bhedabhed vad*, and thus, degrading the Hindu religion and philosophy by all means, he promotes only the western orientalists at each and every step of his writings.

Radhakrishnan's derogatory writings confused millions of good souls looking for the path to God, and thus, he created an opening for the other Hindu writers of the 20th century to follow the same wrong tradition of despising the Sanskrit literature, religion and the ancient history that was planned and designed by the British diplomats to ruin the culture, the religion and the history of Bharatvarsh.

Such was the effect of the writings of the western orientalists and Radhakrishnan on the Indian minds that a great number of Hindu writers like, Surendranath Dasgupta, Hemchandra Raychaudhuri, R.G. Bhandarkar, etc. followed the same wrong trend, and, on the same guidelines, a number of books were written in the last eighty years.

(4) A new trend of anti-Hinduism that has developed in the name of Hinduism.

In the recent years some of the Hindu writers have adopted a new trend of representing a purely atheistic view in the name of Hinduism. Their ideology is totally influenced by the writers like Radhakrishnan, Max Müller and others and their style of representation is devoid of proper respect towards the Sages, Saints and the descensions of God. In fact, their views are totally non-Godly, because they don't believe in the true Divine God Who is supremely Gracious and loving, rather their God is a formless spirit or energy.

A few examples of such publications are: "The History and Culture of Indian People" (11 Volumes) by BVB Bombay, "The Cultural Heritage of India" (5 Volumes) by R.K. Mission, Calcutta; "The Cambridge History of India" (6 Volumes) from New Delhi; "Bhishmas' Study of Indian History and Culture" (15 Volumes) from Bombay; and many more series and individual works.

Although sometimes they ignore the indecent statements of meat eating as said by Max Müller etc., but they use the rest of their derogatory views. For example: Max Müller repeatedly stated in his writings the words 'highest self' or 'supreme soul' for supreme God and condemned the Divine personality of God. Radhakrishnan and others went one step ahead and called God as *spirit* (which is the term of the Bible). They also derogated the supreme Divinity of Bhagwan Ram and Krishn and gave a lot of praise to Buddh whose path is called '*shoonya vad.*'

There is a 'theory of evolution' which tells that an aquatic worm becomes a fish, then a frog, then a reptile, then a mammal, then a dinosaur/shrew, then a monkey and then a human being. The illogicality and the unscientific approach of this theory is self evident. Still, some Hindu writers try to compare this materialistic and unscientific ideology with the Divine descensions of God telling that they are the links of evolution.

There are Divine reasons for the descensions of Matsya (Divine fish), Varah (Divine boar), Kachchap (Divine tortoise) and God Nrasingh, etc. Other descensions of God were in human form out of which **the descensions of Bhagwan Ram and Krishn are the most important as They revealed the true path to God and established *bhakti*.** Kachchap and Varah descensions were in the celestial dimension.

The descensions other than Bhagwan Ram and Krishn were for certain specific Divine purposes. But the descension of Buddh was *only* to show the path of compassion and renunciation and *not* the path to God. So **his philosophy is non-Godly** and there is absolutely no description of any part of the Divinity in that, not even the soul. **Thus, the approach of his philosophy is only up to the subtle mind of a human being (and not the soul), and the existence of the "absolute nothingness" only (and not God). So it is called *shoonya vad* (*shoonya* means nothing).**

Many Hindu writers elevate the personality of Buddh and ignore the absolute Divine greatness of Bhagwan Ram and Krishn. Such tendencies are called transgressions when they draw a parallel between the Divine philosophy of the Upnishads with the theory of Buddhism and try to equalize the Blissful state of Divine liberation (*mokch*) with the *shoonya vad* or *nirvan* (nothingness) of Buddhism.

In the name of Sanatan Dharm and Hinduism they degrade the Hindu religion by disregarding the supremacy of the personal form of God, calling Him super soul or spirit etc. They do not give proper respect to the Vedic Rishis, Sages and Saints, and, calling them sectarians, they totally disregard the teachings of the *acharyas* and *Jagadgurus* whose whole life was a Divine benevolence for every soul of the world. They introduce Bhagwan Ram and Krishn only as historical figures who spread Hindu civilization up to the south and the north of India. See a few specimens of such writings:

(1) "...human beings like Ram and Krishn are given the highest religious status..." "Puranas... have fabricated myths." ("Ways of Understanding the Human Past," *PHISPC Publications*, 2001 pp. 34, 68.) (2) "**Indo-European language was the direct ancestor of the Vedic language.**" ("*The Cultural Heritage of India*" by RK Mission, 5th Volume, p. 14.) (3) "**She (Parvati) became a terrible goddess that had to be appeased by animal and even human sacrifices.**" ("*Vaishnavism... Religious Systems*" by R.G. Bhandarkar, chapter XVII, p. 155.) (4) "**The Upnishads are in fact the legitimate development of that scepticism. People (*brahmans*) in that (Upnishadic) age were by no means vegetarians. They ate flesh freely, not excluding even beef...**" ("*The Vedic Age,*" BVB, Bombay, Book II, p. 472, Book VII, p. 526.)

This is all the effect of the western writers on the Hindu minds that collected the intellectual dirt of the followers of the English regime (knowingly or unknowingly) and tried to smear it on the face of Hinduism in their own intellectual style. Otherwise, how could a true Hindu overlook the Divine greatness of Bhagwan Ram and Krishn Whose loving *leelas* are the soul of Hinduism.

The effect of English education and the derogatory literature introduced by the western writers was so deep and subtle that (to some extent) it reflected even in the publications of great patriotic organizations of India. *For example:* (1) "*Kings and Kingdoms*" (Shriram Sathe) published by Sri Babasaheb Apte Smarak Samiti, Nagpur, mentions that: **the composition of Rigved completed around 2000 BC** (p.viii); **Mahabharat war would have happened around 1900 BC** (p.ix); and **the *kali* era started in 3102 BC** (p. xi). It also tells on p. 24 that the **Devas and Asuras were the inhabitants of the land north of Pratishthan (beyond the Himalayas)**. (2) "*Vishwa ki Kal Yatra (Hindi)*" published by Bhartiya Itihas Sankalan Samiti, defies the Upnishadic philosophy and interprets that: *brahm* represents the 'Expanding Universe' (pp. 33, 34) and *hiranyagarbhah* represents 'Big Bang' (p. 58 to 80), and so on. There are several such fictitious imaginations. (3) Another book, "*Dating in Indian Archaeology*" frequently uses the term '**Vedic mythology**' and says that **the beginning of the Vedic tradition would be sixth millennium** (p. 63, 68). On pp. 122 to 124 it says,

"Padma Puran was composed between 14th and 16th century of Vikram era." "Vishnu Puran... had undergone considerable change before its earliest manuscript of the 13th century was prepared." The publications that have such wrong concepts about Hindu scriptures and Hindu philosophy show how careless we are that we have no time even to learn the truth about the true Hinduism.

A glimpse of total Hinduism

There are five main aspects of Hinduism. (1) **Path of God realization:** It teaches the true and eternal path of God realization which is selfless devotion to God called *bhakti.* (2) **The Divinity of scriptures:** Bhartiya scriptures, like the Vedas, Upnishads, Puranas, Gita and the Bhagwatam etc., are eternal and Divine manifestations, revealed by eternal Sages and the Divine personalities. All the Puranas were reproduced by Bhagwan Ved Vyas about 5,000 years ago. They reveal the actual events that had happened in this *brahmand.* (3) **Supreme Divinity of Bhagwan Ram and Krishn:** Descension of Bhagwan Ram and Krishn reveals the supreme loving Bliss of the Divine world that could be attained by any soul through selfless *bhakti.* It is unlimited times greater and sweeter than the *brahmanand* of the foremost *yogis.* Krishn is the Soul of all the souls, and all the powers and forms of God are established in Him, so He is the soul of Hinduism. (4) **The Divine history:** History of Bharatvarsh also includes the descensions of God, but it is mainly the history of its Sages and Saints and the Divine personalities who lived on the earth planet and helped the souls proceed on the path to God through their behavior, acts, preachings and teachings. (5) **Creation of the universe:** Bhartiya scriptures give detailed scientific accounts of the creation, maintenance and the dissolution of the universe. *All these five aspects together are termed as Hinduism. If someone ignores or neglects any of these aspects and accepts the rest of it, then it is not true Hinduism.*

CHAPTER EIGHT

Science of creation of the Upnishads and the Puranas *versus* the modern sciences of the world.

(1) A review of the most popular scientific theories of the world.

Scientists of the world had no preconceived theory or any definite guideline on which to proceed. Following the principle of trial and error they started working in various fields. Based on their insufficient findings, when they discovered something, they formulated a theory out of their own imagination that it might have been that way. Thus, the actual scientific findings which they discovered out of their hard labor and sincere efforts may have been correct, but the theories that they formulated were based on their imaginations, and their imaginations were conditioned to the limitations of their own understanding. Thus, the theories, that are in some way related to the creation or evolution of the world and are beyond the scope of their direct experiments, are not correct.

1. The evolution theory.

The theory of evolution was originally introduced by the early thinkers and it was further emphasized by Darwin when he first produced his book called the "Origin of Species" in 1859. Later on some more people added their theories to the evolution theory of mankind.

General concept of the evolution theory.

It tells that about three and a half billion years ago some microorganisms like bacteria originated and took the shape of amoeba (microscopic unicellular protozoa), and from that all the plants, trees, worms and animals were evolved. Mammals, birds, fish and reptiles were all evolved from *aquatic worms* about 600 million years ago.

The very first **Primates** appeared about 70 million years ago who were fruit eating, tree living shrews (like mice). They became monkeys around 40 million years ago, apes around 20 million years ago, gorillas around 8 million years ago, and then chimpanzees around 5 million years ago. Then came an amazing change. The semi-erect walking habit of gorillas and chimpanzees changed, their spinal curvature was straightened, proportion of arms and legs was corrected, foot formation was modified, size of the brain was increased, position of the head was adjusted in order to see straight, and, around 4 million years ago, they were transformed into bipeds who could walk on two feet and were called the first **Hominids.** Then final refinements happened. Their dental structure was fully modified and the size and the length of their teeth was adjusted. Their brain nerve cells were increased and it went through specialized development to enhance its capabilities, and between 1,500,000 and 300,000 years ago, they adopted a human shape and were called **Homo erectus.** Between 400,000 and 250,000 years ago Homo erectus evolved into Homo sapiens. By 100,000 years ago they evolved into modern man, and were called **Homo sapiens**

sapiens. They first appeared in Africa and Asia about 100,000 years ago. Then they showed up in Europe around 40,000 to 35,000 years ago, America 30,000 years ago and Australia 25,000 years ago. Their brain size was almost double than that of the gorillas. Homo erectus used hunting tools, made fire and used skin garments. That's the entire theory of human evolution.

The theorists use certain terms to express their process of evolution, like: **natural selection, adaptation, recombination (of genes), genetic drift** and **mutation.**

According to this theory certain walking animals (of the ground) when exposed to sea waters were transformed to dolphins and whales. Some kind of primitive cat (which no longer exists) developed into tigers and lions, but in certain circumstances it remained short and became the modern domestic cat. An unknown 55 million year old skeleton of a big dog-like animal, which they named 'Hyracotherium,' was the first ancestor of all the donkeys, horses, zebras and other hoofed animals; and so on.

❧❧❧❧

Comments.

Now coming to the technical aspects of this theory, you should know that the very basis of the theory is unscientific.

1. The first born one-cell microorganism may only grow bigger but it can never produce sense organs on its own. It is impossible, because it has no such impulse to observe the outside world. Senses are never evolved through the evolution process. The impulse to see or hear or taste or smell or touch is not inherent in the body tissues. They are the natural impulses of a being who already has senses and already has a developed mind.

2. The adaptation or natural selection process can only effect a change in the body color or a slight change in the appearance of the body, like, Japanese, Indians and Europeans, etc. That's all. It cannot tend to create new species. See the human beings around the world in various environmental situations. You can't find a group of human beings who would have started a new human species with a strange body and behavior.

3. Technically the mutation process has a very narrow margin of DNA alteration. So it is unable to create brand new species. It could only multiply the number of species of only one category like the various species of tigers and lions. A tiger cannot produce the species of wolves or dogs or bison, and moreover it is impossible to have any kind of evolution during the ice age which receded just 10,000 years ago. These technical discrepancies crumble the whole theory of evolution. There are hundreds of questions for which the theory of evolution has no answer.

The science of instinct, desire, and *karm*.

The animal world is strictly predominated with their individual inherent instincts related to their eating, mating and living habits. There are no premeditated robbers or burglars in the regular animal world, and there are no such animals who mate with the same sex. So, they don't commit sin or do good deed; they only follow their instincts. For example, they kill but they don't murder. Whereas every action of a human being is followed by his personal will and desire, so it is classified as: evil, bad, selfish, good and devotional; and it is fructified accordingly.

This is the main difference between an animal and a human. A human being is not the consequence of any kind of evolution procedure. He has his own personal characteristics and destiny that could be as great as becoming a God realized Saint. But an animal, no matter how gross or how intelligent he is (from a donkey to the most intelligent being of the animal world, an elephant or a chimpanzee), he is bound to live and die and remain in the animal world until his soul is born in a human family. The working of the animal world is based only on their instincts, and the working of the world of the human beings is based on their personal desires which creates various classes of *karmas* of an individual. Thus, both are entirely separate worlds. They cannot be mixed together.

Still today all kinds of monkeys, apes, gorillas and chimpanzees are found in the world, and sometimes some kind of primitive tribes become extinct and some new tribe may emerge in time. So, if you collect the skulls of all kinds of gorillas and chimpanzees and all kinds of skulls of the primitive tribes of today, you can easily categorize them in a certain order of improvement. But it definitely wouldn't mean an evolutionary development, because they all exist in the same age. *It would only show the racial differences of the same period.* Thus, the findings of the skulls of various kinds and classes of brain improvements and the improvements in the formation of the skull are not the evidence of human evolution which is wrongly taken by the researchers and the scientists. These are the racial differences of primitive, more primitive or less primitive kinds of tribes who lived on the earth planet in the different parts of the world. They still do exist in the modern age in the remote areas of the civilized world in the same country. There is a famous story in Fiji Islands that, about 150 years ago, when the first missionary went to preach Christianity, he was eaten up by the native cannibals of Fiji; and still there are cannibals in Asia, Africa and many other countries also. They also have their body and brain like modern human beings.

❀❀❀

2. General relativity of Einstein.

In 1687 Newton discovered 'gravity' which was simple to understand. He formulated the physical laws and detailed his theory known as the Newtonian physics which is still being used in general classical physics and is good enough to determine the gravitational and astronomical situations of our planetary system and our galaxy.

Einstein.

In 1916 Albert Einstein (1879-1955) produced his major work, the theory of general relativity, in which he presented complex equations that showed the characteristics and the relativity of 'space' and 'time' in various situations. He was a kind-hearted man, did many humanitarian works, believed in the existence of God, played violin for relaxation, was born in Germany and died in Princeton, USA.

He said that time does not always tick the same everywhere in the universe. It ticks much slower where there is strong gravity and it also slows down at extremely high velocity. It means that the time-length of one hour on the earth planet will be less as compared to the time-length of one hour on a larger and massive planet. He said that the space is curved to some extent, which is related to the presence of the density of energy in the universe. His definition of gravity was different than Newton's. He said that gravity is not a force that is contained in the mass; it is the effect of the distortion that is caused in the space-time continuum by the presence of a mass. It means that the existence of a massive object (of any size) creates a derangement in the smoothness of the space and this distortion gives rise to the gravitational force that appears to be coming from the object. His other important aspect of the general relativity was that the light rays do not always move in a straight line. They bend when passing by a star or any planet.

He also mentioned about the black holes which are non-shiny bodies in the space with such a strong gravitational force that even light cannot escape from them. It is absorbed into them. That's why they are called black holes. Prior to his *general theory of relativity* he also produced his *special theory of relativity* in 1905 in which he told about the relation of energy with the matter. He said that matter is a 'form' of energy which may be reconverted into energy. He represented this fact with his famous formula $E = mc^2$, where the amount of energy (E) equals to the mass (m) multiplied by the square of the velocity of light (c2). Max Planck had developed a theory in 1900 that the energy released from the atoms is not a continuum, but rather exists in small quantas (portions). Einstein further developed this theory and said that light is composed of individual quantas (called photons) that have a particle/wave-like dual behavior.

❧❧❧

3. Quantum mechanics.

The quantum theory deals with the behavior of atomic and subatomic particles which have dual particle/wave-like characteristics. Photons, electrons, protons, neutrons, the subparticles like quarks, antiquarks; they all have dual behavior. They are particles or quantas of energy so they act like a smoothly moving particle, but any kind of even minor interference causes them to act in a wavy motion and in an unpredictable direction. There is always some kind of interference in the space everywhere, so there is always an uncertainty in measuring their exact location at a particular moment. Thus, *the fundamental uncertainty of the behavior of the particles* has become the principle of quantum mechanics.

This uncertainty is sometimes quite large. For example: The uncertainty behavior of an electron in an atom is about the size of the atom it is orbiting. It means that it can never be predicted where it would be at a particular moment because it doesn't follow any definite orbit. Inside the atom they behave more like waves, but when they are outside of the atom they behave more like a particle but they are subjected to wave-like behavior at any time. The largeness of quantum uncertainty varies in different situations. Apart from the particles, the composite bodies like atoms and molecules also have a wave-like property and are governed by the same laws of particle-wave mechanics.

Quantum theory predicts that a whole lot of virtual particles may pop up any time in empty space. These particles disappear so quickly (due to the uncertainty principle) that they cannot be measured directly. However, their assumed existence is required for theoretical calculations. These particles always appear as particle/antiparticle pairs in order to conserve all types of charges (such as the common +/- electric charge) and may have every possible wavelength. Such a probability with added uncertainty in the quantum theory makes all the known and unknown particles act, react, and interact in any form and manner and create any kind of energy, or gravitational or anti-gravitational effect in the universe. The quantum theory also predicts that energy itself (in its initial form) may have gravitational or anti-gravitational force, but there is no explicit gravitational theory in quantum mechanics.

4. The hypothesis of the Big Bang and the inflationary theories as postulated by George Gamow and Alan Guth, etc.

In the Big Bang model, the universe expands with violent force. Like a loaf of rising raisin bread, this homogeneous and isotropic expansion spreads its inner concentrated contents all over. But, the description of its *inflationary* aspect is much beyond that. It is a kind of brain-freezing and mind-stretching description of the happenings, and its related figures may scatter the wits of a thoughtful person if he really tries to conceive the logicality of the event. To start with: Try to imagine that after the (Big Bang) Planck time, when the universe was trillions of times smaller than a proton, the energy contained in it may have inflated it to a span of 100,000 light-years, and that also in less than a trillion-trillionth of a second (one light-year = 365 x 24 x 60 x 60 x 186,000 miles).

There are certain technical drawbacks of this theory: How did it start? They don't know. How was it controlled? They don't

know. What was the character and kind of the prime energy? They don't know. Why did it start? They don't know. Why didn't it start earlier? They don't know. And what is the ultimate destiny? They don't know. Like this there are hundreds of questions to which these theories give no answer.

❃❃❃

In 1948 George Gamow with his two colleagues created a theory that the universe began with the explosion or outburst of an extremely condensed matter. They called it 'ylem.' Its density was a billion times more than that of water, and the temperature was 100 billion Kelvin. They called it the Hot Big Bang or Big Bang. This theory was based on the discovery of the constantly expanding universe by Hubble. It doesn't explain at all how it started. After a presumed start, it says what happened after that. Their hypothetical condensed matter 'ylem' was in a 'big squeeze' and it was in an extremely tiny form. The hypothesis of the theory is like this:

1/100th second up to 1 second. The highly concentrated ylem exploded and it began to expand very fast. The particle/antiparticle pairs such as neutrino/antineutrino, electron/positron and nucleon/ antinucleon (neutrons and protons are called nucleons) appeared and annihilated each other to form photons. (Since quarks were not postulated to exist until 1964, they are not mentioned in this theory.) According to this theory there should have been exactly equal number of particles and antiparticles in the universe, and thus, in this procedure, the formation of atoms was not possible, because the formation of the atoms needs variation in the nature, size and the quantity of the particles. (But the observed universe is almost entirely made up of particles only, and this is one of the biggest drawbacks in the elementary Big Bang theory.)

❃❃❃

The inflationary (or the new inflationary) theory.

According to the findings of the scientists, the universe of today has a large scale uniformity to a greater extent in the distribution of the matter, and the second thing is that the 2.7K temperature is found almost everywhere in the observed universe (called the cosmic microwave background radiation) in a homogeneous style. It was the presumption of some scientists that the Big Bang style of expansion of the universe could not have produced such a uniform effect. So, in 1980, a new theory called the *inflationary theory* was introduced by Alan Guth which he presented in a seminar and wrote in his articles in the scientific journals. The main unresolved issue of this theory was that it didn't definitely show how the inflation would stop. Andrei Linde at Moscow University and Paul Steinhardt at the University of Pennsylvania worked on this theory and tried to compromise the inflation problem by modifying the properties of the *hypothetical higgs field.* By 1982 the new or revised inflationary theory was introduced. Since then some more scientists added their revisions and corrections to the theory. The final book "The Inflationary Universe: The Quest for a New Theory of Cosmic Origins" by Alan Guth came out as late as 1997.

The inflationary idea seems to be taken from the blowing of a balloon when a boy excitedly blows it very fast in the beginning but when he is a little out of breath he blows it slowly. The inflationary theory, which is a kind of big insert in the Big Bang theory, cuts in from the very beginning to only a fraction of a second (10^{-36} to 10^{-32} sec.), then it follows the normal Big Bang pattern. It says, *"With the explosion the space was formed, the 'time' started, and the 'space' along with the energy began to expand with a great force."*

In this theory there are a lot of pure speculations in that theory, just like: the *Grand Unified Theory, grand unified force,* the *super force, higgs field* and *higgs particles,* and *false vacuum* (anti-gravitational) energy etc.

There are a number of questions to which the creation theories of the modern science have no proper answer. For example: How could anything appear from pure void? Who created the pure void? Who determined the sequence of evolution (because energy has no mind)? How was the space evolved (because physicists don't accept space as an energy and a 'void' cannot expand or evolve)? Who regulates the safe formation of the galaxies without collision? When there were evenly spread out clouds of gases everywhere in the beginning of the universe, why are there varying sizes and shapes of galaxies? Why didn't they evolve exactly the same way? How and why did these bodies in the space have a different speed and angle of rotation; and so on?

※※※

Comments: The 'Big Bang' and the 'inflation of the universe' never happened.

I will give you a few basic points to show their impracticality.

Gamow, in his Big Bang theory, assumed that an extremely tiny ball of pure neutrons (ylem) just appeared out of the blue, exploded, and became the most sophisticated systematized orderly universe. There is a popular example of evenly rising raisin bread in this reference. Even a child knows that when his mom makes homemade bread, it rises. But there is *someone* to make the dough and then to start the oven. Then, who created the ylem, and who started the explosion and the expansion of the ylem? These are the basic unsolved questions of this theory.

The inflationary theory tells that: (a) The inflation of the space itself contained the prime energy (which can exist at different energy levels from a false vacuum to a true vacuum level). (b) Its energy density (the mass) was 10^{80} grams per cubic centimeter, (c) it had 10^{29}K temperature, (d) it was 10^{-52} meter in size at 10^{-36} second, and (e) that energy density remained constant during the inflation. Every aspect of this statement appears to be bizarre and unfounded.

Unfounded in this sense that it ignores the established laws of the physical science and evades the limits of the particle physics; and bizarre in this sense that it gives such giant figures of subtlety, density and temperature etc., which are beyond the comprehension of a human mind.

Space. Space is an all around continuum existence. It is not formed of any kind of particle. Physical science does not know anything about its characteristics. Even Einstein didn't understand the characteristics of the 'space,' that's why first he added and then he subtracted the cosmological constant term from his equations which was called the biggest blunder of his life. Then how could the theorists say that 'the space' was also evolved as an effect of the first outburst of the prime energy. Space is not such a thing that could be evolved, inflated or stretched. Physicists don't count the space *itself* as an energy, and *no scientist in the world has ever tried to inflate the void/space in his lab* and to shoot an electron within a few meters of space to run for a much longer time than it requires to cross the actual length of the experimental tunnel. The scientists of Princeton Plasma Physics Laboratory have succeeded in generating extremely high temperatures up to about 10^8K as an experiment, but they have never tried to stretch 'the space' in the lab. Then, how is it said that the universe, along with the space, inflated and is still expanding? *This is the first unscientific approach of this theory.*

Heat. *Heat is generated* by domestic means, or through a generative process, or in an experimental lab, or in the space itself by annihilation, or by the thermonuclear reaction of the sun. The heat energy in its initial dormant form is 'no heat' which could be measured. Hold a match box in your hand and you are not burned. Only when you ignite it, then it produces the heat wave and it could be strong enough to burn down a house or create a historical event like the Great Fire of London. You drink trillions of hydrogen atoms in the form of cold refreshing water, but an ignited chain reaction of atomic fusion in a hydrogen bomb could eliminate a small town. So, the heat that could be measured in Kelvin does not exist on its own, it is produced. How did then a 10^{29}K heat temperature exist when there was not a single atom or a photon or even a particle? (10^{29}K temperature is almost a trillion-trillion times greater than the center of a medium size star.) *Such theories defy the laws of the particle physics.*

Cooling reaction. It's a law that heat moves towards the colder region. But if there is no colder region in the vicinity, the heat would maintain its own temperature, it wouldn't drop.

Guth says that *the energy density (of the matter having a mass of 10^{80} grams per cubic centimeter) remains constant as it expands.* Now think of the inference of this statement. **When the energy density remains exactly the same during the inflation, how could the assumed temperature drop?** It cannot.

The mass and the size of the original microscopic universe. Further bewildering is Guth's imagination of the 10^{-52} meter size and the 10^{80} cubic centimeter mass of the energy density of the microscopic universe which he calls the super force. Accordingly, the *10^{-52} meter-* size of the first form of the matter comes to: *a tenth of a trillion-trillion-trillionth part of the size of one proton;* and the *10^{80} cubic centimeter* mass of the same thing comes to: *a hundred thousand trillion-trillion-trillion-trillion-trillion times greater and denser than an atomic nucleus.* Relax a few minutes, and just try to imagine about that unimaginably tiniest thing and its unbelievable mass…, and you will yourself understand the total impracticality of such a creation theory of the modern science.

※※※

The topics of creation and evolution are beyond the limits of human understanding. So, in this reference, whatever would be the product of a material mind, it would always be incomplete. A theoretical astrophysicist at the University of Chicago, David

Schramm says, *"Whenever you are at the forefront of science, one-third of the observational results always turn out to be wrong."* (Time, March 6, 1995, p. 78)

But the question is: When scientists know the shortcomings of their professional findings, and they realize that their means are incapable of probing into the deep secrets of the nature, then why don't they (who speculated the theory of evolution of life on the earth, or the formation of the earth planet and the evolution of the universe) **accept the controlling power of God instead of creating new concepts** like the Big Bang, or the inflationary theory, or a fish becoming a frog and a dinosaur becoming a bird, etc.? Why do they have so much neglect for God when they face a great blockage at every step of their experiments and when their inner conscience itself knows that 'nature' doesn't have a mind of its own so it must be the work of the supreme Divine power (God), because the nature itself cannot manifest such an ingenious creation of the universe on its own?

(2) Creation of the universe and the development of life and civilization on the earth planet according to the Upnishads and the Bhagwatam.*

Aim of creation.

The aim of creation is to give a chance to all the souls to become human beings and then to realize God Who is absolute Bliss. They can realize God by doing absolute good actions and surrendering to Him. Souls are unlimited in number and are in an infinitesimal 'life' form, having a subtle mind of their own. When they receive human body during the creation they do good or bad actions according to the discrimination of their own mind. The record of these actions, called the *sanskars* or the *karmas*, are stored in a section of the mind. The consequences of these *karmas* have to be fructified otherwise there would be no meaning of classifying them as good or bad, and they do fructify. Thus, these collective *karmas* are like a subtle semi-dormant 'force' which reside in the mind of every soul and become the cause of its next incarnation; and the force of the collective *karmas* of all the unlimited souls works as one of the causal forces to create and maintain the universe.

Duration of creation.

The duration of the existence of the universe is countless but not unlimited. It goes on perpetually in a cyclic motion, like the creation state, and then no-creation state. In the no-creation state

---

*Bhagwatam, third canto, chapters 5 to 12.

(called *maha pralaya*) the creative energies and the forces remain in an absolutely subtle and dormant state, and in the creation state they evolve in the form of the universe as we see it today. There was no beginning of this 'cycle of creation and *maha pralaya.*' It is eternal.

Powers involved in the creation.

God inspires the power *maya* (the cosmic power in its absolute subtle form) which evolves itself into the form of the universe and the souls begin to reside in the universe in living form. Thus there are three entities involved in the creation of the universe. They are: God, all the souls, and the lifeless *maya.* God is almighty and absolute-life-knowledge-Bliss. He is omnipresent in His Divine personal form and has uncountable absolute virtues. Just like, He is all-Gracious, all-beautiful, all-loving, all-charming, all-knowing, all-kind and all-forgiving to whoever takes refuge in Him. *Maya* (the cosmic power) is a lifeless miraculous energy or power. It has three characteristics or qualities called *sattvagun, tamogun* and *rajogun* (pious, evil and selfish; pretty, ugly and normal; and positive, negative and neutral) that appear in every part of its creation. Souls, in the universe, are unlimited and are infinitesimal.

Forces that keep the universe running.

There are two forces that keep the universe running continuously. They are 'time' (called the *kal)* and '*karm*' (the accumulative force of the accumulated *karmas* of all the unlimited souls, as described above).

Time (*kal*) factor is not just the elapsed period that we count according to the calendar. Time (*kal*) is an eternal energy like *maya* which is a strong force that starts the manifestation of the *mayic* attributes (which gradually become the universe), and then it keeps the universe moving forward until *maha pralaya*. The time, that we calculate as the age of something or the passing period of an ongoing event, is the calculation of the aging process of something, or it is a point of determining the past, present or future. It is like a parameter that gives you an understanding of the period that elapsed or it helps you keep the record of an event of past, present or future. But the 'force of time' that pushes the universe to move forward is an 'eternal energy' that exists side by side with *maya*.

✿✿✿

Procedure of the creation of the universe.

All the three: souls along with their *karmas, maya,* and *kal* (time), stay in God in an absolutely subtle form and in an absolutely dormant state during *maha pralaya*. They are activated by the will of God. After certain subtle phases of evolution the first thing that comes into being is the endless empty space.

(1) "तस्माद्वा एतस्मादात्मन आकाशः सम्भूतः । (2) आकाशाद्वायुः । (3) वायोरग्निः । (4) अग्नेरापः । (5) अद्भ्यःपृथिवी ।" (तै. 2/1).

There are *seven phases* of extremely subtle manifestations of *maya* that had already happened before the 'space' came into being. (1) Space was the *eighth* subtle manifestation which was, in fact, the first gross manifestation of the energy of *maya*. (2) In the endless space, unlimited number of pockets of various sizes were created. They became the base of uncountable sub-universes. Within that unimaginably enormous and endless-like looking space, the *ninth* phase of *maya* (called *vayu*) was evolved which created a circular movement in the space itself, as if the entire space was in a circular motion from its central point. (3) Then, all over in that space, subparticles evenly emerged. This was the *tenth* phase of *mayic* manifestation (*agni*). (4) Then the subparticles and the particles annihilated to form hydrogen atoms. This was the *eleventh* phase of *mayic* manifestation (*apah*). (5) Then gravity began to predominate and the basic structure of uncountable galaxies and their clusters (as scientists know) were gradually formed. This was the *twelfth* phase. The 'already existing motion' in the space now made it look like the galaxies were moving away from each other. The speed of this motion of the space varied in different areas of this visible universe but with a perfectly controlled synchronization. (The topic of creation is further detailed in "The Divine Vision of Radha Krishn.")

None of the existing theories so far have been able to create such a model of the universe that could accommodate all the features of the known universe. But, this knowledge was already incorporated in the Bhagwatam that was produced by Bhagwan Ved Vyas before 3102 BC. On the basis of the Bhagwatam, we have described this theory in 7 video speeches on the Brahm Sutra that reconciles all the existing problems which the scientists face in forming the model of the universe.

❀❀❀

The functioning of a planetary system.

The supreme God Who controls the creation and the functioning of the entire universe is called Maha Vishnu. When the galaxies begin to assume their normal shape, at that point Maha Vishnu creates a great number of Divinely celestial spaces in the galaxies and He enters into those spaces. He then produces one Brahma in each section who controls the creation of the sun and its planetary system. Thus, in every planetary system there is one Brahma who is called the creator. Prior to the creation of the earth planet, Brahma extends the celestial space and creates celestial abodes of gods and goddesses. One planetary system with its celestial abodes is called one *brahmand.* In this way there are a great number of *brahmandas* in one galaxy. Celestial abodes are invisible as they are in a different space (dimension).

Now we know that the formation of a planetary system is not a coincidental creation of nature as the cosmologists believe, it is a controlled formation. Souls are already in the universe in their subtle form, a certain (uncountable) number of souls are transferred to each planetary system run by its own Brahma, and then, gradually Brahma produces those souls on the earth planet in their material bodies.

᠁

Life on the earth planet.

After the formation of the earth planet, the ozone layer was formed, oceans began to exist, and the first form of life appeared on the earth planet. The Upnishad says that first the vegetation appeared.

How? The soil itself contains the subtle form of the seeds of all kinds of vegetation, like, grass, plants, shrubs, flowers and trees of all kinds. Brahma transfers the souls into those seeds and the first vegetation grows. Afterwards it creates its own seeds. The bodies of insects etc. are produced as a general procedure of the nature and Brahma transfers the souls into them. We know that sometimes in the rainy weather a lot of flying insects are formed in the open space.

Later on, small creatures like fish and birds and then big creatures like tigers and elephants etc. are produced. At this time, Brahma produces the souls along with their body.

One thing must be noted here, that because souls are eternal they must have been living in some form prior to this creation before *pralaya.* Thus, it would be highly unjust if the soul of some human being is by mistake transferred into a worm's body or a worm's soul is transferred into the body of a human being. But you don't have to worry, because Brahma is Graced with the Divine intelligence so he never makes such mistakes.

He produces all the souls exactly according to their previous status **(यथापुर्वमकल्पयत्)**, a grass becomes a grass, a frog becomes a frog, a lion becomes a lion, a human becomes a human, and so on.

So, Brahma produces the first pair of all the creatures big and small on the earth planet. Afterwards they multiply themselves.

One should not think that how did the animals just appear on the earth planet, or was there some kind of evolution process involved in that. The impracticality of the theory of evolution has already been discussed. The most significant thing is this, that when a Divine personality Brahma who is so powerful, that he creates the whole *brahmand,* maintains the entire planetary system, and remembers the identity of each and every living being of the earth planet from each and every bacteria to an elephant and all the human beings as well, then there is no reason that he can't create the bodies of the animals. So he does, and thus, the first creation of the animal world was done by Brahma.

God Vishnu, God Shiv and creator Brahma.

(3) The exact calculations of the age of Brahma and the existing *manvantar* according to the Bhagwatam.

Absolute age of the earth planet and the sun. Bhagwan Ved Vyas explains in the Bhagwatam that 155.52 trillion years have passed since Brahma originally created this planetary system, and this is the present age of Brahma.

The Bhagwatam says, "Brahma's one day equals to 1,000 cycles of the four *yugas* (one cycle of four *yugas* is 4.32 million years). It is called one *kalp*. There are fourteen Manus in one *kalp*. For the same length of time there is the night of Brahma. This is called *pralaya* or *kalp pralaya*. At that time the earth planet and the sun along with three celestial abodes *(bhu, bhuv* and *swah)* enter into the transition period (and become uninhabited). During that period Brahma holds within himself all the beings of the material and the celestial worlds in a suspended state and sleeps. (The next day he again produces them and re-forms them as they were before.) In this way Brahma lives for two *parardh* (twice of 50 years). After that, there is a complete dissolution of the *brahmand* (the planetary system and its celestial abodes). This is called *prakrit pralaya* of the *brahmand*." (Bhag. 12/4/2 to 6)

"Half of Brahma's life is called *parardh*. One *parardh* is finished and the existing *kalp* is in the beginning of the second *parardh* (the first day of the 51st year of Brahma). The very first day of Brahma was the day when he himself was created by God Vishnu and it was called the *Brahm kalp*. The present running *kalp* is called *Varah kalp* (or *Shvet Varah kalp*)." (3/11/33,34,36)

"In this *kalp* six Manus like Swayambhuva Manu etc. have elapsed. The **seventh Manu** is the son of Vivaswan. He is the present Manu and is called **Vaivaswat Manu.**" (8/1/4; 8/13/1) One *manvantar* is: 308.57142 million years. Thus, 1851.4285 (6 *manvantar*) + 116.6400 (27 cycles of four *yugas*) + 3.8931 (the three *yugas* and the elapsed time of *kaliyug*) = 1971.961604 million years in 2002. This is the existing age of the earth planet.

In the Bhagwat *Mahatmya* Bhagwan Ved Vyas reveals a great secret and says that **this is the 28th dwapar (of Vaivaswat manvantar).** Not in all, but sometimes at the end of the 28th *dwapar* of a *kalp* the supreme personality of God, Krishn, in His absolute loving form descends in the world on the land of Bharatvarsh and reveals His supremely charming playful Divine *leelas*; and that had happened in our age just about 5,000 years ago. (Bhag. Ma. 1/ 29)

According to the above information, Brahma's age which is also the absolute age of our sun and the earth planet is: 50 years of Brahma x 720 days and nights x (1,000 x 4.32 million years of the four *yugas*, which is one day of Brahma) + 1,972 million years (the existing age of the earth planet) = 155.521972 trillion years.

One year of Brahma is of 360 days (and one month of Brahma is of 30 days). So, 360 x 50 = 18,000 days and nights of Brahma have elapsed. Thus, our earth planet and the sun have already been renovated 18,000 times. **It's a big figure, but reasonable if you think over it deeply, and again it is given by an all-knowing Divine personality.**

(4) Actual age of the universe.

Now come back to the topic of the age of the universe. A scientist may say that stars in the universe are up to 14 billion years old, whereas medium size stars could be 8 to 12 billion years old, and the age of the universe could be 15 to 20 billion years old. But, is it the age of the total universe? No, because the universe also contains black holes and the neutron stars whose age is not added to it. Paul Davies in his book **"The Last Three Minutes"** (published 1994 by Basic Books, Harpers Collins, New York), describes about astronomers' understanding of the fate of the stars. He says,

> "Nobody knows how many stars have already succumbed in this manner, but the Milky Way alone could contain billions of these stellar corpses… A *dwarf star at the bottom end of the stellar-mass range may shine steadily for a trillion years."* (p. 46)

Taking this view of a dwarf star's life into consideration, the actual age of the universe jumps from the range of billions of years to trillions of years. Again, think of a dwarf star changing to a neutron star, and a neutron star turning into a black hole. It may easily come to several trillion years. And then, how long these black holes have been in existence, no one knows. **Thus, it could be reasonably believed that the universe must have been existing for hundreds of trillions of years.**

It could be further believed that when *these* black holes were in the shape of the stars, the configuration of the clusters and galaxies of the universe of that period may have been different than it is observed today.

Again, if you consider the universe of *that* period (when the existing black holes of that period were the stars) there must also have been black holes in the cosmos of *that* period, because the existence of the black holes is the procedural factor of cosmic-mechanics.

In this way, going backward and backward, you will find that *the true life of the universe comes to uncountable trillions of years,* and it is a fact that, according to this procedure, the configuration of the cosmos would have perpetually kept on changing from one black hole period to another black hole period which was always in the range of trillions of years. **Thus, considering uncountable trillions of years as the total age of the universe, the figure of 155.52 trillion years as the total age of our *brahmand* is not very much.**

❀❀❀

Now we understand that our history is not the history of triumphs and defeats of worldly kings and queens who entangled themselves in fulfilling the needs of their passion, and our scriptures are not mere theories or ideologies of material minds which are incomplete by their own nature. Our scriptural writings are the direct Divine manifestations revealed by the Divine minds of our great Saints, and the major part of Bhartiya history is the history of eternal Sages and Saints and such Divine personalities who descended on the earth planet to show us the path of eternal happiness that has no limits. They revealed the scriptures to give us an understanding of the deceptive illusions of the world and the unimaginable Blissfulness of God Who is the true friend of every soul of the whole world.

Do you know?

- That the fully developed Ganges valley civilization has unceasingly existed for 1,900 million years.

- That the Ganges valley civilization survives during the 'ice ages' whereas the other civilizations of the world don't. How?

- That the prime scriptures of Bharatvarsh are Divine powers that were originally revealed trillions of years ago.

- That the current age of our sun and the earth planet is 155.52 trillion years, and the sun has consumed its fuel and re-energized 18,000 times. This fact is unknown to the scientists.

- That the universe is not only 20 billion years old but it is *uncountable* years old.

- That the Sanskrit language has been in its perfect form since its introduction in the world.

- That the Valmiki Ramayan, relating the history of Bhagwan Ram, was written 18.144 millions years ago.

- That the Upnishads primarily relate and sing the glory of the Personal form of God, *not the impersonal (nirakar)*, and *only* one verse of one Upnishad (out of 108 Upnishads) describes the true characteristic of *nirakar brahm*.

- That the historical descriptions of the Upnishads and the Puranas relate to three dimensions: material, celestial and the Divine.

- That even the oldest languages like Hebrew and Greek were in the primitive stage of formulating and stabilizing their alphabet around 900 BC, but we have definite documentary evidence of the public recitation of the Bhagwatam in 3072 BC.

- That all the human civilizations of the world were at some time the distant offshoots of the original inhabitants of Bharatvarsh.

- That the ancient masterpieces of the western world, like Iliad, Odyssey, Beowulf and Dionysus etc. relate to the lust, jealousy, cruelty and revengefulness of their imagined heroes, gods and the barbarous people of those days.

- That the source of the myths of the world and Homer's imagination of mythological gods originated from the broken stories of the Puranas that travelled to these countries through the trade routes by word of mouth.

- That the words used for god in Hebrew, Greek and Latin languages only meant 'to invoke,' 'to call,' or 'the luminous one' and they were used to indicate some kind of celestial being or power.

- That there is still no concept of Gracious God in Hebrew and Greek languages.

- That the fictions of 'Proto-Indo-European' language and 'Aryan invasion' were originally introduced by Sir William Jones whose associates fabricated and adulterated certain portions of Bhavishya Puran and our Vedic ritualistic books etc. in a demeaning style.

- That Max Müller was given very high wages for translating the Rig Ved in a misleading way.

- That even Einstein was perplexed by the mystery of 'space' (when he dropped his idea of 'cosmological constant'), and that the black holes hold the secret of the age of the cosmos.

- That the *big bang, inflation, evolution, continental drift* and *the expanding universe* are only speculated theories, formed out of incomplete scientific data.

- That even after 100's of years of speculations the physicists of the world have not been able to determine the current 'model' of the universe up till today, which the Hindu scriptures, the Upnishad and the Bhagwatam, have already defined and detailed in 12 step-wise system of creation of the universe.

- That Bhartiya scriptures give the true historic chronology of trillions of years since this *brahmand* (the sun, the earth planet and the celestial abodes) was created by Brahma whose current age is 155.521971961604 trillion years (in 2002).

All of this and much more, with historical, logical, scriptural and scientific evidences, is in –
"The True History and the Religion of India,"

which also gives the world history of the social developments of 8,000 years; and, in a sequence, it relates the most valuable theme of all of our scriptures which are a Divine treasure for every soul of the world who desires to receive the love of God. They are: *4 Vedas, 4 Upvedas, 6 Vedangas, 4 Kalp Sutras, 6 Darshan Shastras, 11 Upnishads, 18 Puranas, Ramayan, Mahabharat, Gita and the Bhagwatam.* It also describes the philosophy and the teachings of the *Jagadgurus, acharyas, rasik* Saints and the prominent Divine personalities of the last 5,000 years.

Endorsements for "The True History and the Religion of India"

"The True History and the Religion of India, A concise Encyclopedia of Authentic Hinduism," Graciously authored by His Divinity Swami Prakashanand Saraswati is one of the most comprehensive books on human civilization. It is an authoritative view of the history of world thought. The book provides the most valuable information and knowledge on the Vedas, the Upnishads, the Gita, the Bhagwatam, the Puranas and all of the Hindu religion and thought. It also gives a comprehensive idea of time as envisaged in the Vedas. It can lead to a good understanding of Hindu history, philosophy, religion and Vedic sciences.

Shree Veera Raghavan, *(Ex) Regional Advisor, Social Development, United Nations; Director, Bharatiya Vidya Bhavan, New Delhi.*

The Divine truth revealed in "The True History and the Religion of India" is so amazing that it would prove to be the infallible arrow of this age to destroy the non-truthful and misleading comments about Hinduism... Without studying this book it is impossible to imagine, that how the unlimited knowledges of Bhartiya scriptures and world books were incorporated into one single volume? It is amazing; and is *truly an incredible miracle of the genius world.* (Translated from Hindi)

Shree Tarun Vijay, *Editor, Panchjanya, New Delhi.*

This amazing encyclopedic book, revealing the authentic history and the religion of Bharatvarsh, *is truly unique and unparalleled.* (Translated from Hindi)

Shree Bhanu Pratap Shukl, *author and journalist, New Delhi.*

This epoch-making book "The True History and the Religion of India" is designed for sincere research scholars and the seekers of God's love. His presentation of the western theories is amazingly logical and abundantly admirable. He has allowed the western theories to speak for themselves.

Shree Vachaspati Upadhyaya, *Vice Chancellor, Shri Lal Bahadur Shastri Rashtriya Sanskrit Vidyapeeth, New Delhi.*

In our opinion this is *the first book* that has put together vast information about the history of India, Sanskrit language, Vedas and Upnishads, the planetary system and the development of human civilization.

Dr. Vijay Kuchroo, *Professor, Harvard University, Cambridge.*

In recognition of the true revelation of the authentic knowledge of Hinduism, "The True History and the Religion of India" by **His Divinity Swami Prakashanand Saraswati** (*for the first time in 400 years*), the supreme council of the World Religious Parliament, New Delhi, India, which is comprised of respected spiritual teachers and Vedic scholars, celebrated the joyous occasion in Ficci Auditorium and awarded him the Spiritual title of **"Dharm Chakrvarti"** (Spiritual Master of the World) on April 11, 1999.

※※※

This is an encyclopedic book which traces the history of various civilizations and countries in relation to the history of India. The religion of the Indian civilization, the Sanatan Dharm (the eternal order) is discussed in extenso. The book is a mine of information.

Dr. E.C.S. Sudarshan, *Professor, University of Texas, Austin.*

※※※

I am much pleased to receive a copy of "The True History and the Religion of India." This work encyclopaedic in nature will be of great use for historians, research scholars and those who desire to know about the true history, religion and culture of Bharatvarsh.

Jagadguru Shankaracharya Shree Jayendra Saraswati Swamigal, *Kanchi Kamkoti Peetham, Tamilnadu, India.*

Jagadguru Shankaracharya of *Dwarika Sharda Peeth* and *Jyothishpeeth*, Swami Swaroopanand Saraswati has expressed his hearty appreciation for the monumental work by His Divinity Swami Prakashanand Saraswati "The True History and the Religion of India" which is an authentic book on Hinduism.

※※※

194

(Endorsements from topmost scientists of the world)

"The True History and the Religion of India" is a comprehensive exposition of the basis of Hinduism. This book has made an admirable start in incorporating the ideas from Hindu scriptures to expand on the recent scientific findings. They are very thought provoking. However, because of the seriousness of the subject matter and the depth of each topic covered, this book should be read as a text.

Dr. Gautam Badhwar, *Chief Scientist for Space Radiation, 'Exceptional Scientific Achievement' Medalist, Johnson Space Center, NASA, Houston.*

In my experience of about 30 years at the Jet Propulsion Laboratory of the California Institute of Technology I had not yet read such a clear, smooth and brief description on the theories of evolution, origin of the universe, and the general theory of relativity. It is amazing to realize that Swamiji has such a depth of knowledge of the subjects in which people spend their entire career. His conclusions about the inadequacies of these theories are based on logical arguments that are very convincing. This book is a must for reading by those who are wanting to be enlightened about life, its role, and how it should be lived.

Dr. Santosh Kumar Srivastava, *Fellow of the American Physical Society, Principal Scientist, JPL California Institute of Technology (NASA), Los Angeles.*

The Vedas, Upnishads, Puranas, Darshan Shastras, Manu Smriti, Mahabharat, Ramayan (Valmiki and Tulsidas), Bhashyas on Brahm Sutra, Bhashyas on Gita, the Bhagwatam, Shat Sandarbh, and other books by the *rasik* Saints, etc.

There are thousands of Bhartiya scriptures as described in Part 2, Chapter 3 of "The True History and the Religion of India." They were revealed and written by the Rishis, Divine personalities, *Jagadgurus* and the *rasik* Saints. Only the most important ones are shown here.

Contents
"The True History and the Religion of India"

Chapter 2

History of the origin and the development of the languages of the world; and the origin and the development of Greek, Roman and western religions and civilizations from 4th millennium BC to 20th century AD 95

Chapter 3

The eternity of the Sanskrit language; the diplomatic schemes of the British during the 18th, 19th and the 20th century to destroy the culture, religion and the history of Bharatvarsh; and its effects on Hindu writers

Chapter 4

The words of Krishn Himself; evaluation of the most popular theories of the world; continuity of Bhartiya civilization for 1,900 million years; and the general chronology of Bharatvarsh of 155.52 trillion years 405

PART - II
Chapter 1
Twelve phase creation of the universe and the history of our *brahmand* as described in the Bhagwatam

Chapter 2
The references and the events described in the Puranas and the Upnishads relate to the entire *brahmand*, and not only the earth planet

Chapter 3
The theme of all of the prime scriptures and the Divine personalities of 5,000 years

Chapter 4

Sanatan Dharm is the universal religion of the Upnishads, Gita and the Bhagwatam which Bharatvarsh has introduced for the whole world

Glossary

acharya. A historical descended Saint in whose name a religion is formed.

bhakt **Saint.** See Saint.

bhakti. Devotion, adoration and loving remembrance of Radha Krishn (or any other form of God) without desiring any worldly thing from Him.

Bhartiya. That which relates to Bharat (Bharatvarsh), which is the original name of India, like Bhartiya philosophy.

brahm. It is a common word for any form of God, like *brahm* Krishn.

brahmand. A planetary system, including the earth planet, sun, moon and all the celestial worlds up to the abode of Brahma.

braj ras. The Bliss of Radha Krishn *leelas* that generally all the *Brajwasis* experience (His playmates, mother Yashoda and also the *Gopis*).

Brajwasi. The people of Braj (the Mathura district) who lived during the time of Krishn. *Wasi* means dweller. So *Brajwasi* means the original residents of Braj.

dharm. In general, *dharm* means the religious discipline for the four orders of life. It is called *samanya dharm.* General *dharm* also includes the social disciplines and code of conduct according to our scriptures. It is also called *varnashram dharm* or *apar dharm.* The *dharm* that takes a soul to God is called *par dharm* and it is only selfless devotion to God, called *bhakti,* with wholehearted faith and confidence.

God. The supreme, all-powerful Divinity, Who is kind, gracious and omnipresent in His Divine form in His entire creation, and also has an omnipresent impersonal aspect of His Divine being. It is equivalent to the word *bhagwan.*

Gopis. The maidens of Braj during the descension period of Radha Krishn.

Gwalbals. The playmates of Krishn.

gyan, gyani. The followers of impersonal aspect of God are called *gyani* and their impersonal concept and understanding is called *gyan*. See also: Saint.

kaliyug. The age of materialism, which is the existing one.

kalp pralaya or *pralaya.* The partial destruction of the earth planet when the sun grows and becomes so hot that everything is burned on the earth planet. This is the transition state at the end of every *kalp* when the three celestial abodes *bhu, bhuv* and *swah* are destroyed.

karm. Thought and action of a person.

leela. The Divine action of any kind. The pastimes, sports, plays and all the actions of Radha Krishn are called *leela*. All the actions of a Divine personality (God or Saint) are Gracious and Divine.

maharas. Once Radha Krishn fully revealed Their Divine love on a particular Sharat Poornima night (5,000 years ago), while playing, singing and dancing with Radha Krishn. That was *maharas*.

manvantar. The second biggest cycle of time which is of 308.57142 million years. The current *manvantar* is called Vaivaswat *manvantar.*

math. The building of the main center of the religious propagation.

maya. The original cosmic (material) power that manifests the whole universe. It is lifeless so it has no mind of its own but it works in a very systematic, computerized manner. It has its own inherent qualities called pious, impious and devilish (*sattva, raj* and *tam*). *Mayic* means, that which is related to *maya*, or is the product of *maya*.

nikunj leela. The *leela* of Radha Krishn where only *Gopis* associate. (Thus, all the *leelas* of Divine Vrindaban are the *nikunj leelas*.)

nirakar brahm. The formless aspect of God which is established in the personal form of God (and all the personal forms of God are established in the personality of Krishn).

raj, rajas or *rajogun.* It is one of the qualities of *maya*. See *maya.*

rasik **Saint.** See Saint.

Saint. The one who has visualized and realized God in any form, and whose teachings are based on the themes and the guidelines of the Gita, Bhagwatam and Upnishads which are our prime scriptures. There are three categories of Saints: *gyani* Saints, *bhakt* Saints, and *rasik* Saints. (1) *Gyani* Saints are those who have attained the impersonal (*nirakar*) form of God. They are of two kinds: *gyani* Saint and *yogi* Saint, (2) *bhakt* Saints who attain the (Personal) Divine love form of God like, Vishnu, Durga, Shiv, Ram, Krishn, etc. (3) Those *bhakt* Saints who attain the Divine love form of God like, Ram or Krishn are called *rasik* Saints (*ras* means the Divine love), but generally speaking the *rasik* word refers to those Saints who have received the vision and Divine love of Radha Krishn.

sakar or **sakar brahm.** It means the all-virtuous personified form of God. *Sakar* is the main form of God and, with the *sakar* form, He/She is omnipresent with all the Divine virtues such as: Graciousness, kindness, all-Blissfulness, all-lovingness, and many more.

samadhi. The ecstasy. The quality and the depth of a *samadhi* depend upon the *sattvic* purity of a devotee.

Sanatan Dharm. The eternal (*sanatan*) universal religion. It contains the knowledge for the spiritual well-being of all the souls. It provides the guidelines for all kinds of people of the world, which, if followed, leads them towards God realization.

sanyas. The renounced order of life meant for the service of God and God realization. The one who takes this order is called *sanyasi.*

sattva, sattvic or **sattva gun.** The pious quality of *maya.*

tam, tamas or **tamogun.** See *maya.*

yagya. Vedic ritual with fire ceremony.

yog. It is the eightfold system of very disciplined form of meditation which is described in the Yog Darshan of Sage Patanjali. Its aim is to neutralize the mind from all kinds of attachments, attractions, likings dislikings and loving emotions, and then to enter into thoughtless *samadhi.* It has to be practiced to seek union with the impersonal (*nirakar*) aspect of God by surrendering to a personal form of God in order to receive the liberation from the eternal bondage of *maya.*

yogi. The one who practices *yog* is called *yogi.*

निखिलदर्शनसमन्वयाचार्य, भक्तियोगरसावतार, भगवदनन्तश्रीविभूषित
१००८ जगद्गुरु श्री कृपालुजी महाराज
Nikhiḍdarshansamanvayàchàrya,
Bhakṭi-yog-rasàvaṭàr, Bhagavaḍananṭashrivibhushiṭ
1008 Jagadguru Shree Kripaluji Maharaj

Literature: *Revealed by Bhakti-yog-rasavatar, Jagadguru Shree Kripaluji Maharaj*

प्रेम रस सिद्धान्त
(Prem Ras Siddhant)
The miraculous philosophical book that describes the true path of God realization along with the philosophies of all the scriptures and the *Jagadgurus*.

प्रेम रस मदिरा (Prem Ras Madira)
1,008 songs (*pad*) of Radha Krishn *leelas* and devotional humbleness.

भक्ति शतक (Bhakti Shatak)
One hundred couplets describing the eternal greatness of *bhakti* as described in the Brahm Sutra, Gita, Upnishads and the Bhagwatam.

राधा गोविन्द गीत
(Radha Govind Geet)
(Part I and II) Eleven thousand one hundred eleven verses describing the total philosophy of "Shat Sandarbh" and "Bhakti Rasamrit Sindhu."

युगल शतक (Yugal Shatak)
A new series of one hundred chantings related to the name, virtues and the *leelas* of Radha and Krishn.

युगल माधुरी (Yugal Madhuri)
Soul-enticing chantings related to the loving blissfulness of Radha Krishn.

युगल रस (Yugal Ras)
Short and simple lovely chantings of Radha Krishn.

श्रीकृष्ण द्वादशी तथा श्रीराधा त्रयोदशी (Shree Krishn Dvadashi and Shree Radha Trayodashi)
Twelve *pad* describing the decorations and the beauty of Shree Krishn and thirteen *pad* describing the fascinating beauty and decorations of Radha Rani.

ब्रज रस माधुरी
(Braj Ras Madhuri Part I and II)
A collection of over 300 Divine chantings of the name, form and virtues of Radha Krishn.

प्रार्थना एवं आरती
(The Prayer Book)
Prayers, *arti*, homage and devotional instructions for daily devotion as explained by Shree Maharajji.

Books written (or translated and elucidated) by H.D. Swami Prakashanand Saraswati

Jagadguru Shree Kripaluji Maharaj (Teachings and His Mission)

It gives a brief account of the life history of Shree Maharajji, his teachings and his Gracious manifestations in the form of Divine literature and Spiritual Centers.

Prem Ras Madira

Translated in English, are the selected songs of Prem Ras Madira that were revealed by the supreme Divine descension of this age, Jagadguru Shree Kripaluji Maharaj.

The Divine Vision of Radha Krishn

An elucidation of the topics of "Prem Ras Siddhant." It incorporates the philosophy and theme of more than 400 scriptures and gives a crystal clear view of the devotional path.

Science of Devotion and Grace

An expanded version of "Prem Ras Siddhant" in English detailing each and every aspect of devotion, God realization, the qualities of a true Spiritual Master and the Grace of God.

Sanatan Dharm

It is a summarized version of the philosophies of our prime scriptures (Upnishads, Puranas, Gita and the Bhagwatam) and all the *acharyas* which form the body of Sanatan Dharm.

Bhakti Shatak

One hundred couplets revealing the philosophy of Brahm Sutra, Gita, Upnishads and the Bhagwatam and detailing the prominence of *bhakti* which is the only true path to God realization.

Yugal Shatak

One hundred chantings of Barsanewari Radha Rani and Krishn which Shree Maharajji wrote when he was in Barsana during Guru Poornima in 2000. They have been translated into English.

Braj Ras Madhuri

The chantings in this book are revealed by Jagadguru Shree Kripaluji Maharaj. Their general meaning is described in English.

Leela Madhuri

This book was designed especially for English knowing devotees. Chantings and *pads* have been translated with word for word meanings. It also contains a Hindi to English dictionary of common words.

The Prayer Book (Hindi and English)

Prayers, *arti*, homage and devotional instructions for daily devotion as explained by Shree Maharajji.

The Philosophy of Divine Love

English translation of "Prem Ras Siddhant" by Dr. Bageeshwari Devi.

The Divine Teachings

- ◉ Dear friend! Do you know that your inner self is yearning for such a 'love' that could extend the happiness of your mind to a non-ending limit and make your heart blissful forever.

- ◉ That '*love*' is neither a feature of your own mind nor a quality of this mundane world. That is Divine, and that is God Krishn, Who is all-attractive, all-charming, all-beautiful and all Blissful.

- ◉ Radha is the Soul of Krishn or you can say that Radha's other form is Krishn, so the all-Blissful and all-charming beauty of Krishn is, in fact, the eternal charm of Radha. Thus, Radha Krishn are Both one in two forms.

- ◉ You should know that sensual engagements ignite desires that sooner or later end up in disappointment. A beautiful thing never remains beautiful forever. It wilts, ages, and fades away. Every relation in the world is insecure, because every person keeps on changing his mind, less or more. Then what is so good on earth? Yet your mind thinks it is charming, because it is conditioned to its own intellectual fallacies.

- ◉ It is thus an illusion under which people live, remain hopeful for their whole life, and find nothing.

- ◉ No one else can help you come out of this intellectual fallacy. You yourself have to understand it. It is all so evident and obvious in the practical world that you don't need any other evidence since you have already witnessed many disappointments in your life.

⦿ Once you have tasted the sweetness of the devotional love of Radha Krishn, your whole being will be thrilled with joy. It is such a 'joy' that starts in the heart, develops in the heart and stays in the heart, because heart is the seat of Krishn love.

⦿ It is such a 'feeling' that has no definition and it is such a 'happiness' that has no limits. It is something that includes everything your soul needs, and it is the only thing your soul has always desired.

⦿ So what are you waiting for? Don't waste any more time and surrender yourself to Radha Krishn. 'They are truly yours and you belong to Them.' This is the only feeling that you have to strengthen in your heart and mind to experience Their closeness.

⦿ Shree Swamiji says that human life is precious. Don't unnecessarily waste it running after the illusive pleasures of the world. Use it for God realization that could make your life Blissful forever.